The Boy and the Big White Rock

First Edition

A MEMOIR

Jerome Mark Antil

Copyright © Jerome Mark Antil 2024

ISBN: 979-8-9886448-3-5
(Paperback Edition)

Library of Congress Control Number: 2024918244

This book is based on real events. Though true, oral history of passed down dialogues are naturally fictionalized because of fallible memories.

A special thank you to
Diane Simowski

No part of this publication may be reproduced, stored in a retrieval system, or transmitted in any form or by any means electronic, mechanical, photocopying, recording, or otherwise, without the written permission of the author or publisher.

To my first lady—

Pamela

My mother and father—circa 1920

Chapter 1

"You can't make this stuff up!"
~ Bart Simpson

My name was changed at gunpoint—it became Jerome Mark Antil. I'm a writer.

I was in my sixties birthing a writing career when it happened. I had flown from Dallas to Los Angeles to chat with a publicity intern with a Hollywood firm. The intern's responsibilities included clipping articles about clients like Brad Pitt and Jennifer Aniston and standing on the red carpet, giving the show's producer a heads up on arriving limousines as celebrities stepped out. While there, I was a houseguest in a sprawling Spanish hacienda overlooking Hollywood on the crest of Laurel Canyon with friends, food service executive Webb Lowe and his beautiful and talented wife, Ruta Lee a celebrated Hollywood Walk of Fame star, actress, and dancer in major hit movies, with supporting roles in countless television shows and a leading lady on stage. Among her thousands of performances, Ruta Lee had co-starred in the movie *Sergeants 3* starring Frank Sinatra and his fabled Rat Pack of the 1960s. After shooting wrapped, Sinatra and the "guys" named Ruta Lee an official Rat Pack member.

Following my two-day visit, I needed to get to the airport, LAX. The plan was that an intern would come and drive me to the airport. The time came and went, and there was no answer on the intern's phone.

"I'll call a cab," I said.

"Hold on, Jerry," Ruta said. "Webb and I are going to Palm Springs for the weekend. We'll leave now and drop you at the airport on our way."

"I don't want to put you out," I said.

"Nonsense, but we'd better hurry if you're going to make your flight," Ruta said. "Everybody, in the car. Webb, you drive."

We were pulling down the long, curving driveway to Laurel Canyon Boulevard when my phone rang. From the front seat, Ruta, with raised voice:

"Is that the intern calling?"

"It is," I said.

Ruta's hand reached behind her head with a loud click of her finger and thumb.

"Give me the damn phone," Ruta said.

I put it in her hand.

"Honey, if it was Jennifer in our back seat right now, you'd be in some deep shit," Ruta said. She handed the phone back to me. The intern apologized for oversleeping and having the phone turned on *silent*.

We pulled up to the terminal. I got out and grabbed my bag as Ruta lowered her window.

"Thanks, guys," I said, "for the hospitality, good times, and for the ride. I love you both—above and beyond."

"Jerry, darling—bye, bye—or as Frank would say— 'Fuck you very much!'"

I grinned and turned up the steps into the airport.

I always went by Jerry—everyone knew me as Jerry—but that moniker was about to be erased without warning as a uniformed officer grabbed my arm and forcibly pulled me out of a baggage check-in line.

"Come with us, sir," the officer said. I reached for my suitcase. Another officer grabbed my other arm to restrict my movement.

"Leave the bag, move this way."

They steered me into a holding room with a stainless-steel table in the center. One of the officers locked the door behind him, and with a hand resting on his holster, said, "Step out of your shoes and move away from them."

"What!?"

"Do it now!"

I complied.

"Now stand back against the wall," barked the other officer.

I obliged.

"Remove your clothes," one officer said.

"Are you serious?" I asked.

"No talking!"

"All of them?" I asked.

"Strip to underwear and socks," the other officer said.

He repeated for me to take off my coat, shirt, tie, and pants, and toss them on the table. If I tried to speak, their hands would offensively grip their weapons and one would repeat the bark that I wasn't allowed to say a word. This nightmare lasted for more than an hour before a third officer unlocked the door from outside, poked his arm in to see me alone in the room, tossed my shoes on top of my clothes on the table, and summarily dismissed me with an uncaring, blank face.

"You can go."

On my way out I inquired as to what I had done.

"It's Saturday, this is LA, you're wearing a suit."

"That's the reason?"

"Your driver's license says *Jerome*, your ticket says *Jerry*. We're required to check incongruities."

"Why'd you take my shoes?"

"The suit could have been a masquerade for the dress shoes. We check shoes for bombs."

From that moment on, in a changing America of the new millennium, I've been inclined to adopt my given name, Jerome, everywhere but at the dinner table.

Why am I telling you this?

As I grew older, I learned that the only things we really get to own and keep in life are our memories and it's those moments, for better or worse, that impact and shape our lives. There are fond and happy memories and there are the darker memories too, like my LAX experience.

The story I'm about to tell isn't just about a boy who grew up from the second grade through the eleventh grade in the lap of comfort in a large home on an inspiring eighty-four-acre estate in upstate New York—and was forced in his senior year of school to move with his parents and two siblings 788 miles away, sleeping on a canvas cot in a small, one-room apartment in the poorer lower-east side of Milwaukee, Wisconsin.

That happened in 1957, but while my candle still burns, there are two persons of character, my mother and my father, and what I've grown up thinking was a dark circumstance I found myself in during my senior year in high school—a situation that has deeply affected my life. I only recently discovered I've had the facts of what happened and the circumstances that surrounded them wrong all these many years.

I've learned what really happened to my parents at the time—not to me or my brothers, but to my parents—and what my parents chose to do about it, and how they kept it to themselves. The story I recount here began unraveling when I was 15 years old, sixty-eight years before I started to write the sentence you're reading now. It has taken a large wedge of my lifetime to discover the truth, its meaning to my parents' legacies, and how it will forever change what I've grown old wrongfully remembering as a traumatic, unhappy ending for my parents oh so many years ago. I'm a writer because of my parents' examples and guidance, and I'm blessed that I can take newly discovered truths and weave them into this final tapestry my parents deserve.

Chapter 2

"A transition period is a period between two transition periods." ~ George Stigler

In 1755, my father's great grandparents were driven out of Normandy and his grandparents then again from Nova Scotia in a political purge. They ultimately settled in Acadia—St-Jean-Por-Joli, Quebec, Canada. Other Norman French deportees of the time migrated to New Orleans as Cajuns. It would be the next generation—my father's parents—who would legally migrate from Quebec to America, through Minnesota.

It was there my father, Michael Charles Antil, was born—the seventh son of a seventh son of a seventh son. He would grow to be a tall, ebullient sort, quite likeable, quick witted, insatiably curious and always with a smile and an offered hand. As a teen he was a popular babysitter, tall-tale storyteller, and a swimming instructor at a posh casino resort on one of the many lakes of Minnesota.

My father at eighteen, in North Dakota.

THE BOY AND THE BIG WHITE ROCK

As he grew to six-foot-six, taller than his six older brothers while still in his teens, he would walk hundreds of miles to the Dakotas and drive four-horse teams pulling thrashers throughout the wheatbelt of America and sleep under the stars. At seventeen, while working for a telephone company and installing a phone line in a large three-story bakery in Wadena, Minnesota, my father mentioned in passing to the bakery owner that he should consider painting his bread trucks white instead of the black they were. "Mothers buy bread, Mr. Regan, and they think of milk and white as pure," my father told the baker. So impressed with my father's natural gift for marketing, Mr. Regan had all his trucks painted white and hired him to head up his bread sales.

By his late teens in the early 1900s, my father was a respected giant in the baking industry, and in more ways than one. Because of his extraordinary height and being called a 'giant' on a daily basis—my father believed perception was reality and he made certain he had custom tailored suits made to enhance his presence as he walked into a store. He had such an impressive talent for brand awareness and bread sales to grocers that the W. E. Long Company, a sales and marketing consulting firm in Chicago specializing in retail bread and baked goods sales, hired him to travel the country to consult with wholesale bakeries like Regan Bakery. My six-foot-six father, in his late teens, was paid $50 a day in the early 1920s—at a time most grown men were earning $25 a week or less. Before he was twenty-one my father had stepped in each of the forty-eight states.

His gift of knowing retail bread sales (and his extraordinary height) made him a giant in the baking industry.

My mother's grandmother migrated to America from Ireland during the potato famine in 1845. My mother, the love of my father's life, was a six-foot tall, full Irish blood, illegitimate love child, born in Cincinnati in 1902. Children born out of wedlock in those days drew scorn, and she was adopted by her blood mother's married sister and her husband, who lived in Minnesota.

My mother at 12, in an ice show.

In her early teens she became both a competitive speed swimmer and a professional figure-skating champion, performing for a traveling ice show in the early twentieth century.

My mother and father met at the age of 18 and were married at 20. On their wedding day, my father gave my mother the keys to a fully paid-for new Ford Model T. It was a statement to both her mother and her adopted parents of his ability to support her in proper fashion.

My mother was an inquisitive, intelligent woman who would ultimately raise and formally educate eight children before going to university herself in her mid-sixties, where she'd earn a Master's degree, and would work on her PhD well into her eighties. My mother was a voracious reader. She read a book a week, starting at the age of 12.

My mother and father were devoted to each other their entire lives. When my father traveled on business, he'd sit in his hotel room and write my mother every day. His work ultimately took them to Los Angeles, where their first child was born. They moved to Chicago and then to Hoboken, where my father became vice president of the largest bakery in the world, specializing in hot dog and hamburger buns for the Yankee Stadium and Ebbets Field stadium baseball games, Madison Square Garden events, and horse racing tracks in metropolitan New York City, while mother gave birth to their second, third, and fourth child. At the dawning of the Great Depression in 1930 when nearly 33% of the nation was unemployed and going hungry every night, my parents moved to Cortland in upstate New York. My father had contracts with the federal government to produce bread for upstate soup kitchens and bread lines for the poor and hungry. My father and his partner, Albert Durkee were able to use the government contracts to finance their bakery. Without commercial electricity available at the time, the largest bakery in the area was limited to baking forty-two loaves at a time. At age 29, with six children in tow my father and Albert Durkee were able to buy electricity from a private generator owned by the village streetcar company. With an electronic oven so large it took three weeks to preheat, they cofounded one of the largest independent bakeries in the world baking 82,000 loaves of bread a day. Throughout my earlier career, I earned my living writing marketing and research plans. I discovered baking was a very profitable industry. I did the math. I remembered my father once telling me a bakery was lucky to make a penny a loaf profit. A penny a loaf profit during the Great Depression baking 82,000 loaves of bread every day, 365 days a year would have yielded a today's equivalent of five-million-dollars-a-year in profit.

The wholesale baking business was a 24-hour-a-day enterprise. My father relished the energy it took and the satisfaction he got when someone picked up a warm loaf of bread, smelled its aroma, and smiled. For a break in their week and for some alone time away from the kids, my parents would leave the children with a trusted friend, Agnes Odessa, and go on Sunday drives into the country.

One of these Sundays took them 24 miles away from Cortland, where they happened upon a curious property that got their attention. There was an arching banner over its driveway entrance that read DELPHI FALLS PARK. The property looked abandoned. There were two pavilions set back about a hundred yards from the road. One of the pavilions was for storage and one, the larger of the two, was an empty hall, as if for public events, such as meetings or dances. They were both boarded up. Behind the pavilions was a row of twenty-four brick fireplaces with cooking grills facing a sixty-foot-high waterfall. There was a steep hill on the right of the waterfalls where hand-hewn timber steps led up to a level cinder path on top. One could walk a path through woods on that side to the top of the first (lower) waterfall, over it to the upper waterfall behind the first.

My father learned the park had been built in the 1920s by FDR's CCC (Community Conservation Corps). The CCC and other Roosevelt works programs were created by the president to help men keep their dignity by earning a fair wage for a fair day's work, and to be fed and housed. The only thing the government asked these men in return was that they send all but $2 of their pay envelopes to their home and families each week.

My parents' imagination saw them turning one of the pavilions into a home for their growing family—eight of us at the time, currently living in a three-bedroom house. In 1939 they bought the property—eighty-four acres, two waterfalls, two pavilions and a small stable.

That same year, threats of America being drawn into a war in Europe halted the purchase of nonmilitary or nondefense building material. Their dream had to be put on hold.

Therein began the saga of my parents' fortitude and drive. Ever-positive, they decided to have a family Sunday powwow at the falls. After Mass at St. Mary's in Cortland, they packed their six children in the car and drove to their Delphi Falls Park for a family picnic. My father moved a picnic table close to one of the cookout fireplaces and patiently stoked a fire for a mound of hot dogs while Mother poured lemonades.

"Mommy?" my father asked. In front of the children, my father always called my mother *Mommy*.

"Yes, dear?"

"It's looking like President Roosevelt isn't getting much support from Congress on our helping England and France out of the pickle they're in with what's going on over there with this Hitler guy, and now Mussolini—" my father started.

"It's frightening," Mother said.

"Talk is we'll be in the war soon enough—least that's the talk. We can only pray."

"Will it be World War II, Daddy?" my sister Mary asked.

"Looks like it," my father said. "England doesn't have enough money to fight it alone. They're going to need all the help they can get—money, ships and planes—and men. No telling how long this one will take."

"What's on your mind, Mike?" my mother asked. "You wouldn't have brought this up in front of the children if you weren't thinking something."

My father turned and pointed his cooking fork back to the pavilion behind them.

"Mommy, we can't move into that pavilion for a spell—what with the War Act—but I was thinking why let this beautiful place go to waste?"

"What's on your mind, Mike?" my mother repeated.

"Mommy, what say you and the kiddos put your heads together and turn this pavilion, these fireplaces, the trails through the woods, the waterfalls, everything here, into a money-maker? We can put it in the bank for their college money. How about it?"

"But we live 24 miles away," my mother said.

"I don't see that as a problem," my father replied.

"Run it from Cortland?" my mother asked.

"Think about it, Mommy. We're only talking Saturdays, Saturday nights. You bring the kids out early Saturday morning—give them each a job—let people come see the falls and picnic on Saturdays. Saturday nights you have a live band play music, fancy round dance, and they could even call square dances. It'd be a regular Saturday night jamboree."

"A learning lesson for the children," my mother said.

"Can we, Mother?" my sister Dorothy asked. "Can we, please?"

My father handed out hot dogs and ears of corn.

"Little peanut," my father asked my sister Dorothy, "What job do you want?"

"Can we have a pet zoo, Daddy?"

"You'll have to ask your mother, Peanut. Mommy's the boss—this is her show."

"Mike," my mother started. "You could get those donkeys you used while making that sign on the Preble Corner hill—maybe a baby lamb or two … and a Tom turkey might be docile."

From that moment on, with my mother at the helm, a family enterprise, Delphi Falls Park, was reborn.

Mother would drive the kids twenty-four miles to the falls every Saturday morning. They would lift eight shutters and brace them open with poles, prepare the dance pavilion, and shave wax chips on its floor. My mother hired a regional band, the Round-Up-Riders, and square dance caller to entertain folks with an evening of round and square dances.

Throughout the day, my sister Dorothy would stand guard with a local man Mother paid to stay with her by the petting zoo—two donkeys, Dot and Dash, and one baby lamb.

Eldest teen sister Mary would dress in western garb and a cowgirl hat and sing with the band. Mother learned music management and she would book the group—in return for plugs promoting Delphi Falls Park for Saturday picnicking and dance—to sing on the radio for 15 minutes two mornings a week on WHCU in Ithaca.

My sister Mary would leave the radio studio and my mother would drive her to school at St. Mary's Catholic in Cortland.

At the Saturday night dances, my brothers Mike and Fred took turns selling tickets and rubber-stamping hands at the door or got behind the refreshment counter and sold orange drinks and potato chips. The Saturday night round and square dances at the Delphi Falls Park were a diversion for locals from the toils of farm chores and the fears of war coming to America—especially when it did finally come by taking their sons away from them. My mother ran everything, even though back then it was unprecedented for a woman to be thought capable of managing a business on her own. She ran dance ticket sales, the food concessions, and the music management. My mother was an example to her daughters and to her sons. That's just the way it was in the Mike and Mary Antil household.

In 1941, two years after they purchased the Delphi Falls, I would be born, becoming their seventh child. In 1943, Jim would be their eighth.

Chapter 3

"Take a method and try it. If it fails, admit it frankly, and try another. But by all means, try something." ~ Franklin D. Roosevelt.

"God help us if man ever lets that war be redundant—God help the world if we haven't learned from it," my father said. The war had been a costly nine years in lives lost and money spent, but it ended in 1945, and with it, the War Act ended, and my parents' dream of life in the country became a reality. Other than Saturday picnics and dances, the pavilions had been vacant, boarded up and unheated every cold winter month for nearly a decade.

Snow collapsed the pavilion roof.

Both roofs finally gave in to a heavy snowfall and collapsed. The smaller pavilion collapsed completely; the larger pavilion only had a corner damaged and was repaired and reinforced. In 1947, the few of us who were still living at home moved to our new country home—Delphi Falls. It had been such a long wait for the war to end, by the time we did move, half of my siblings were in college or married.

I was six when the car with me in it first pulled into the drive of our new house. I was seeing Delphi Falls for the first time. My father parked behind the set of swings that were once a part of the park. I got out and stood, listening to the magical blend of the endless roaring from the waterfalls and the quiet sounds of the country. I remember thinking how peaceful it sounded.

Stepping inside the house for the first time got your attention. If you've ever smelled rotten eggs, you'd have a sense of what water from a sulfur bed smelled like. When my father had the well dug under the pavilion, they hit a bed of sulfur. It was healthy—my father would tell us people paid good money to swim in sulfur baths or to drink it—but until you got used to the rank odor that would leave your nostrils praying for plugs, you'd turn your head and hold your nose just to turn a faucet on in the sink.

Rotten egg smell aside, our first day was about moving things in, organizing our rooms (I was to share a room with my brother Paul), and helping my mother with boxes meant for the kitchen cabinets. Stepping outside to try to breathe fresh air helped, but we eventually got used to the smell. That first night we went to bed with all doors, front, side and back, opened wide, letting the air in and letting the sulfur smells out. Opened doors were also my parents' statement of how safe and peaceful the country was. They knew in time we wouldn't smell the sulfur.

The first morning I woke earlier than the others. It was one of the few times I hadn't wet my bed. I ventured down the hall into the living room, where I was startled to find a wild animal on the living room floor. It was small, but it had a frightening, almost pre-dinosaur look about its head, with bulging eyes and a pointed snout with long rows of threatening teeth on pink gums. The creature's tail was long and hairless, and it curled side to side like a whip. I remember feeling the intruder was young, like me—and thinking it could be rabid and it could attack and bite me out of fear. I made myself busy grabbing and stacking sofa cushions around the creature, hoping to trap him.

I went into the kitchen, opened the icebox and poured a saucer of milk. I topped it like a mad scientist in a laboratory with sprinkles from every spice jar I could reach in the cabinets without my pajama bottoms falling down. I placed the saucer with the milk and mélange next to the creature and cautiously backed away to go in to wake my father. When he came out the animal was gone. Its tail left a long, wet line of milk on the linoleum floor from the saucer to the opened back door. My father smiled, went to the bookshelf by the fireplace and pulled an encyclopedia volume out. He opened it to a page to show me an opossum.

"That's it, Dad," I said. "That's it!"

My father smiled. "That's an opossum, son."
He pointed at the picture in the encyclopedia.
"Was he as big as this one, son?"
"Smaller. I think he was a baby," I said.
"That little guy was more frightened of you, Jerry."
"He was?"
"This was his turf, son. Now we're his neighbors."

Throughout the next thousand or so days my memories of my adventures at the waterfalls behind the once boarded-up pavilion that became our home were the most magical. That sixty-foot-tall wall of shale we called Delphi Falls would always be my imaginary bookend to a shelf full of stories of friends, farmers, and farm families I would grow to know.

The farms on this magic rectangle shelf ranged in size and stretched from the high hilltop of Cazenovia and then southwest and down to the valley bottoms below, over our falls and up again to Gooseville Corners, then west over twelve miles of rolling hills, through Fabius, the village where our school was located. Apulia Station was next (little more than a train depot stop), then on to the town of Tully on Route 11, my other imaginary bookend. Then north on Route 11 from Tully eight miles to the town of Lafayette and then right on Route 20 and back to Cazenovia—seventeen miles east—passing through Pompey and Pompey Center, where Winston Churchill's mother was raised, and then down a long, steep hill past the Snow White Inn to Oran Delphi Road and up the other side, an even taller Cherry Valley hill, through Moore's Apple Farm.

Every hill was carpeted with emerald green pastures or red apple orchards or by dark green tree tops. The farmers were blessed living in such a rainfall, winter snow-rich area. Together, small farmers in that magic rectangle I affectionately dubbed as "the crown," in my historical fiction books managed a combined 3,200 milk cows. A good part of the milk and butter New York City's milkmen sold and delivered came from our area's farms. The refrigerated train car was invented in Syracuse to haul milk in iced, insulated tanker train cars 230 miles from Apulia Station down to New York City every day.

There was a shared sense of awe in our waterfalls, the Delphi Falls, as if this had been a mystical place long before we arrived.

Most kids in the day would entertain themselves reading, whether lying on the floor reading the full newspaper page or two of illustrated comics in daily morning and evening newspapers. I remember once thinking how lucky it was that our home was in the Cazenovia township, birthplace of the classic, *The Wizard of Oz*, and where Mark Twain typed his *Adventures of Huckleberry Finn* on the world's first mechanical typewriter—a Remington—not far away, in Elmyra, New York.

I found comfort with a whispered, hypnotic, continence the metronome of shushing sounds the lower and upper waterfalls kept time with. There was a meditative quiet when I'd hike trails through the woods. In years to come I would appreciate how the hills of upstate New York were the inspiration to a number of poets and authors alike. Henry Wadsworth Longfellow's *Evangeline* spoke of the Acadians (my ancestors) and their expulsion from Normandy and Nova Scotia by the English. It was as if Washington Irving's *Legend of Sleepy Hollow* could have been inspired in these beautiful hillside climbs from the reality of daily life. To most who had stood and watched them, especially the locals, the Delphi Falls would always be a pleasant memory, even if they only saw them once or twice, perhaps during a courtship picnic or cooking on one of the brick fireplace grills. Or, perhaps while kneeling at the falls to propose marriage or posing the family to take some Kodak photos to frame over their mantels back at their farms.

As for schooling, my mother insisted on two simple principles. First was that her children would learn music, so they could be exposed to the arts. Second, learning about life in a country school would benefit children far more than their learning about life in another urban environment. So, Mother opted for us to go to a rural school. Our home was in Madison County, but the school my mother wanted us to go to was in Onondaga County. It was a conundrum. Until things were sorted, my mother made her statement by delivering me for my first day to a one-room schoolhouse a mile away in an Onondaga County hamlet, once named Delphi, now named Delphi Falls. In it there were six rows of desks, each row representing a grade, one through six.

Then one day, almost magically, a school bus pulled to a stop at our front gate and honked. Mr.

Scullens (Ralph) added our home to his daily stops and welcomed us aboard. He carried my brothers and me to the 300-student first through twelfth grade Fabius Central School in the village of Fabius. In time, my mother became president of Fabius Central School's PTA. In the postwar 1940s, my mother, Mrs. Cerio, and other women from Fabius created an actual night school at Fabius Central to benefit returning veterans pulled away from their farms and educations to serve in World War II.

In our family, I was the seventh child of a seventh son of a seventh son of eight siblings. Our mother and father made us ten: Jim, Jerry, Paul, Dick, Fred, Mike, Dorothy, Mary, Mom and Dad. My mother and the local women who rallied with her were amazing. Among other things, they brought the first doctor into Fabius—Dr. Brudney.

2nd Grade – I'm 3rd from right – bottom row.

At Fabius Central I became one of 43 kids in Mrs. Heffernan's second grade, which was next door to the school library and two doors from the school principal's office, Mr. Young.

I had always been a quiet child, not speaking before I was four. In Cortland's St. Mary's Catholic School's kindergarten, I was so frightened I'd wet in the sandbox. I was leery of the Franciscan nuns and rumors of reform school at five, so I chose not to speak in the first grade as well. If someone in the classroom talked without permission, the sister (nun) would threaten to hang a thread of yarn around their neck from which a paper cutout of a long tongue hanged. It could have been that or worse, having to wear the dunce hat that lay in wait on a stool in a front corner of the classroom.

For me, moving to the country was a breath of fresh air. It seemed a gentler, kinder place. I no longer had the harsh daily ritual of having to go into a Cortland funeral home and kneel in front of dead people, like my first-grade nun had me do when I was five.

Chapter 4

"Art can never exist without naked beauty displayed." ~ William Blake

I had finished my first week in the second grade at Fabius Central School, and I felt good about the transition. It was a sunny Saturday, no one was at home, and I decided to run out to the waterfall naked to wade under the falls.

I didn't know how to swim, so I'd look about in wonder and pick up small fossils lying about on the shale shoreline over on the cliff side of the falls. I'd imagine myself having conversations with the crawfish, the birds, and the tiny minnows in the shallows under stones at the foot of the falls. I'd see crawfish scurrying to safety under rocks in the creek. I'd go from watching minnows swimming to the cliff-dweller swallows flying in and out of clay nesting holes they'd carve in the taller-than-me cliff on the creek bank's clay side. I'd stare at water droplets starting at the top of the waterfalls and my eyes would follow them dropping down into splashes.

    Unbeknownst to me, while I was enjoying Mother Nature on this outing, my mother had come home from whatever errand she was on and Mrs. Heffernan, my teacher, had stopped by for a cup of tea. After my trek to the waterfall, I ran barefoot and bare-naked to the house and jumped through the open screenless door into the living room of what I thought was an empty house to find my mother and Mrs. Heffernan sipping tea. I remember their awkward smiles, and my trying to convince myself without looking down that they couldn't see that I was naked as I turned and walked away and around a hall corner to my room.

    While they poured tea, I could hear them.

    "Mrs. Heffernan, I'm afraid my Jerry still isn't much of a talker," my mother said.

    "Not to worry, Mrs. Antil. In the Christmas play coming up Jerry can be the master toy maker with a no-speaking part. All he'll have to do is stand and pretend to wind up the toys one at a time," Mrs. Heffernan said.

"The *Nutcracker*?" my mother asked. "How beautiful."

"Not quite the ballet, Mrs. Antil, but sort of a musical with children dressed as different mechanical toys. They will all get wound up by Jerry before they make their stage walk-across to Christmas music."

After Mrs. Heffernan left the house, my mother took me to Cazenovia to get me outfitted for the Christmas play. On Saturdays and then again on Sundays after church I'd look forward to donning my new Buster Brown shoes, my train engineer hat with brim, and my new denim bib overalls. I'd break in the stiffness of my overalls by walking down to the road by the gate and then to the bridge. The bridge had a three-foot-tall concrete wall on either side of the road. I'd sit on the side nearest to our alfalfa field across the creek from our house. I'd listen to country sounds and take in the sights—the crackling of a creek, the twirl of leaves when wind rippled through trees, the cawing of crows, geese honking, and the gentle mooing sounds from pastures across the road and up the hill. I'd stare up at the woods on top of the cliffs and wonder if there were bears or mountain lions up there.

"Jerry, try not to get your overalls dirty. It's your costume for the Christmas play at school, and we want them to look nice," my mother said.

I tried my best, but while climbing down to the creek under the bridge I slipped on mud, fell on my butt, and slid down. My mother didn't say a word. She smiled and put them in the washing machine. She gave my shoes to my father to take into work with him and have them cleaned and polished at the shoeshine parlor on Main Street in Cortland.

In the second grade I was a crier. Didn't know why—just was. Still am. Still don't know why. Only difference between then and now is now I'm not the bawler I was back then. It was during that Christmas play's big finale, when everyone was on stage and I was standing deep stage left in my train engineer hat, my bib overalls and dungaree shirt with a red bandana tied around my neck, that every performer on stage began singing in verse:

My Bonnie lies over the ocean,
My Bonnie lies over the sea,
My Bonnie lies over the ocean,

It was right when they were at *"Bring back my Bonnie to me,"* I was crying like a banshee with more tears than there was water over the waterfall behind our house, bawling like a baby seal so loud my denim shirtsleeves were soaked. Mrs. Heffernan had to come from backstage to stand in front of me as a muffler so I wouldn't drown out the singers' second chorus.

My heart sank when I was told the Christmas play was to run two nights. The second night, Mrs. Heffernan had me hold my kerchief in my hands to muffle my mournful bawling.

In time I began to open up, to talk, and make some friends. I was developing a wonderful curiosity in minutia. I found out that the term *next door* had a different meaning in farm country than it did in the city. In the country, *next door* didn't mean a house so close you could talk back and forth through open windows, like in the city. In the country, next door meant a farm or house up the road or down the road and each farm or house could span fifty or more acres with quarter-mile-long driveways. Thing was, country neighbors—whether on small farms, on big ones, or just in a house—rarely had time to leave their place. In the country, going for long walks was standard growing up fare. I'd walk Cardner Road with my brother Paul from our house a mile to Don Chubb's house. He was in my brother Paul's grade.

I was learning that farm families had one thing in common. They worked from early morning milkings before sun-up until well after nightfall, when they'd get to their house, eat, and get to sleep, bone-tired. The work ethic of this life was why most farm families' social life, other than church go-to-meeting days, would be the result of always having a seat at the table in case neighbors dropped by. Neighbors were welcome to sit a spell, eat, and chat. Country folks knew that. Sometimes, a farmer would stop his truck or tractor and visit by pulling over just to say hello to another farmer. As for us kids, our friendships were mostly kindled on school bus rides. We'd share news and gossip to and from school and sometimes we'd be entertained by a showoff kneeling up in a seat, pontificating as if they were selling legends in a bottle. Some families still didn't have telephones at home, and the country didn't have television's infrastructure back then, so the school bus to and from school, the playground at recess, or the cafeteria was where we'd keep in touch.

Chapter 5

"I remember the 1940s as a time when we were united in a way known only to that generation. We belonged to a common cause—the war." ~ Gene Tierney

The postwar forties and early fifties had a fresh smell of positivity about them. It was as if we could smile and mean it for the first time in a long time. It was a time of celebration, not only for having won the war against the scariest enemies worldwide, but for recognizing that what the Allies accomplished created a sense of promise—set an example for all. For America, it nurtured a pride in our sense of public responsibility, morality, and imagination. We were entering a time of renaissance—in people's creativity and inventiveness. The aura was being swept in by returning veterans who had stared personal death and the destruction of entire cities in the face for four years and only wanted to celebrate being alive.

With the distractions of the 50s, adults distanced themselves from the war, but for the young, it wasn't easy to forget what we had seen on Saturday mornings on the movie theater's newsreels or listened to at home on frightening war newscasts on radio. My friends and I witnessed rationing when we were three, four, and five—shortages of food, sugar, and coffee. There were no new tires during the war. Rubber was needed for the military—for the airplanes, trucks, and Jeeps. No automobiles were built in America during the war, either. The steel was needed to build fighter planes, bombers, battleships, submarines, and merchant cargo ships. Thousands of Jeeps and tanks were needed to stop Hitler's Nazi Germany and Hirohito's Imperialist Japan from taking over the world.

The war caused the death of 80 million people, and we watched it on the newsreels. Gasoline was rationed. Stickers on car windows told how many gallons a car was allowed—maybe three gallons a week per family.

I could remember seeing Army, Air Force, and Navy uniforms everywhere I looked around Cortland, especially at the train and bus depots. American flags draped the funeral home next to St. Mary's Catholic School when caskets with fallen soldiers, sailors, or Marines lay inside. Kids listened to the war sitting on the floor in front of a radio, hearing about bomb raids and the war from London or from the South Pacific. We could turn the dial on our Zenith radios to the short-wave bands and sometimes pick up a haunting ship to shore Morse Code message.

In the country, it was as if I could see a rainbow from my school bus window. After my first few rides I began to feel a calming tranquility, a comfort, just watching people we'd pass by returning to their normal lives. It was then I began to believe it was true. The war was over. It was a thing of the past, and it was important we'd never forget its purpose and resolve. But we could move on.

I was witnessing for the first time in my life a brand-new world—not at war—from a window on a bus #21 traveling through James Fenimore Cooper's Leather

Stocking Region of Central New York. The bus would glide along level valley roads with rich brown plowed fields on either side, and after getting a bit of a run while passing the Delphi Cemetery, our bus would climb in a geared-down, determined chug up the hill like a *little engine that could* to the top and a new level plateau, and on to school in Fabius.

My imagination was stirred with every bus ride. I'd absorb the sights and sounds in a reverie. School Bus #21 had become my private train car ride through a museum of life. From any window I might see a lone farmer in the middle of a field, sitting tall on the front of a manure spreader, tugging the reins of a team of horses, fertilizing a plowed hayfield, and another farmer, two farms away, on his knees mending a broken plowshare.

I might see our egg man, ol' Charlie Pitts on his horse-drawn buckboard, trotting down Delphi Falls Road or on Pompey Hollow Road with tied corn stalks in the back. Passing by the Barber farm, I might see a ringed-nosed bull mounting a heifer. Around a bend I watched a man back from the war with only one leg walking with a crutch and carrying a bucket from the milk barn to the house. Up top of Cook's hill, two tractors in tandem disked a long, flat field, preparing it for the planting season coming up.

The hills at Moore's Apple Farm inspired my imagination of Johnny Appleseed legends, and as we'd pass by, there might be ladders leaning on a half-dozen trees with folks climbed up, picking apples. I'd keep a sharp eye out and watch for a farm's secret signals I learned from farmer Barber. If I saw a large red ribbon tied to a tree limb near a farm, I knew the ribbon was a *hobo* signal to other hobos walking by that the farm was friendly and you'd get properly fed for a day's work and you wouldn't be cheated. Hobos were men and one of the results of nearly twenty years of depression and dust bowls, and a loss of confidence. Hobos weren't bums. They were itinerants looking for a better life, looking for a job.

      Examples of good character that one would be lucky to learn in life, I learned riding School Bus #21. From my bus window I learned what hard work went into the preparation, the seeding, growing, and nurturing of plants and animals. I learned how animals were fed during the summer when there were pastures and crops growing and how they ate during the winter, when there weren't crops growing and the pastures were covered in snow. I learned what could be accomplished when families came together to pitch in and lend a hand—to help a neighbor raise a barn, to dig a well, repair a roof. I learned what community spirit meant by watching a dozen or so ladies carrying covered dishes into a small house where someone had passed—showing love, respect and giving community support and relieving the family from having to prepare food during their time of mourning.

Chapter 6

"He is rich or poor according to what he is, not what he has." ~ Henry Ward Beecher

There was nothing as fun as feeling your toes sink into warm powder while walking barefoot on a well-worn cow path that would stretch around and over pasture hills. The paths were just wide enough for the cows to walk in and worn to a softer than sand powder by their hooves. There was never a burr or a pebble on the path. It was comforting knowing that the cows knew that every cow path eventually led either to a rich green pasture for grazing or back to the barn for milking, which comforted them as well. They would line up on the paths when the farmer called for them. One behind the other, they'd mosey down the paths to the barn, twice a day.

Rural kids, not in our teens yet, had a number of things on our minds—like walking on cow paths, chewing on a piece of straw—but money wasn't one of them. Oh, we'd hear our older kin talking of making their first million before they were thirty, but to us, we mostly wanted good friends, to play some ball, to hike the woods or go horseback riding, or crawl through a barbed wire fence without snagging our shirt.

We had our own definitions of rich. To us, rich was a feel-good, a special thing more than it was a money thing. To us, rich was a fulfillment, like walking a path and finding a four-leaf clover or stopping and crouching down to watch a yellow spider spin a web or a beaver building a dam. Some kids maybe thought my family was rich because we had a waterfall, but to put that in context, Bob Holbrook and his eleven sisters and brothers didn't have a water heater or a bathtub in their house, and most times Bob only got a ketchup sandwich and a green apple in his lunch sack, but we thought he was rich because he had three waterfalls we could slide down barefoot behind his house on Berry Road. Bobby Penoyer got a snow sled for Christmas and his parents were so poor they couldn't afford the sled's pull rope until his next birthday, but we thought he was rich because he had the best sledding hill in the area in back of his house and barn.

"Bobby, why's your porch light flashing on and off?" I asked.

"Must be it's getting late," Bobby said.

"Do I have to go home?" I asked.

"No. Mom's making grilled cheese sandwiches and tomato soup," Bobby said.

"Sounds good," I said.

"It's getting dark. She just wants us to come in."

I thought Jimmy Conway was rich because their barn was on the corner of two roads and his father had a Minneapolis Moline tractor. I thought the Dwyer's were rich because their silo had a shiny top made from the new invention called aluminum, and I thought the Barbers were rich because they had a bull with a ring in its nose. Fact was, after the war, most kids I grew up with lived in our own special world—a world that lived through and witnessed the tail of the Great Depression and then an entire world being at war, and all we wanted was to put it behind us. Randy Vaas's father couldn't buy tires to go to work during the war, but Randy was rich because he got to ride in his pop's diesel truck milk can hauler on weekends. I thought the Barbers were rich when Dale Barber called our house and told my mother I should come over to their farm right away. My brother Dick drove me over and we watched a calf being born.

Our small world was as simple as there was food on the table or there wasn't food on the table, but we wouldn't go around all day wasting time quantifying. We knew what doing without was. We knew it when we saw it and we never thought twice about stepping in to help. A hot lunch at school was a quarter. The first day I met Bob Holbrook, I saw him looking through thick glasses into his lunch bag. I could read disappointment in his face from my times during the war.

"What's in the sack?" I asked.

"My lunch," Bob said.

"What's for lunch?" I asked.

Bob tried to shrug me off.

"What's in your bag?" I asked.

"Sandwich, apple," Bob said.

"What kind of sandwich?" I asked. With a sense that I wasn't going away, Bob held his hand over his mouth to muffle the words.

"Ketchup," Bob whispered.

We both lived through the war. We knew what hunger looked like. Hunger was a kid's lunch sack with ketchup or sugar sandwiches. Fed kids had quarters for hot school lunches. I pushed my quarter into his ribs.

"I love ketchup sandwiches," I said.

"What?!"

"Trade you even up," I said.

"For real?" Bob asked.

"Even up," I said.

Bob smiled. We became best friends that day, and we traded every day the entire time we went to school together.

During my school years at Fabius Central, we lived pretty much like farmers. We had some acres; we had a waterfall behind the house; we had three horses and a Karakul lamb that ran off wild into the woods the day my father brought him home. We had some chickens, geese that would chase us up the driveway like watch dogs, ducks, and two Guinea hens that got away and dug up Mrs. Parker's vegetable garden so often my father told my brother Paul to butcher them.

"Do I do it like the chickens?" Paul asked.

"You could, if you can catch them, son," my father said.

My father was right. Paul couldn't get close to them. Guinea hens waddled like they had full diapers but they were fast and could take flight a few feet at a time. Paul finished the job with a .22 rifle and we ate them that Sunday. They were leathery, like chewing on a failed catcher's mitt with grape jam. My mother was the politest about it. She called them gamey.

Chapter 7

"There are three kinds of lies: lies, damned lies, and statistics." ~ Mark Twain

In all my years at Delphi Falls, I had little reason to suspect we were rich. I never got an allowance.

This is an important point. I never got a new bike in my childhood at the falls. In ten years, I only got one used bike, and the tag on it read $3. It was from a bicycle store in Cortland and the pedal clanked against the frame so loudly cows would look up from grazing and back away from fences when I pedaled by.

One Saturday, in 1949, after sitting in the Cazenovia movie house next to the Lincklaen House Hotel, I watched John Wayne in *Around Her Neck She Wore a Yellow Ribbon* three times. It was about the old horse cavalry—I became so in love with Olivia Dandridge (Joanne Dru) when I got home I borrowed my father's paint brush and his window trim paint and painted my bicycle yellow. I'd ride it down to Maxwell's on the corner every week and spent two hours push mowing their lawn for $1.50. My mother made me put half of that in the bank for college.

I never thought for a second we were money rich. I had to walk a mile down to the corner and up the hill to Charlie Pitt's place and back every week with a basket filled with eggs. That was a chore, not a paying job. Home chores like these and cleaning our rooms on Saturdays were a responsibility. My other house chore besides getting the eggs was making desserts—sheet cakes, pies, bread puddings, or a custard. The rule was I had to make something that would last a week of school night suppers. My father taught me how to bake when I was ten. I knew how to use a double boiler and could whip and bake a meringue topping for lemon pie before I turned eleven. I knew a sheet cake would serve more people than a layer cake.

If you sense the times and values for kids my age, without spoiling my end story, you need to know that even though my story picks up when I was ten, it won't be until I'm 15 that I had reason to attach *any* significance to our house, the waterfalls, where we lived as being well off—money rich—to live there.

Why would I?

My folks bought the place before I was born. How could I have known anything about it? Then the year I was born, Pearl Harbor was bombed and all hell broke loose—two wars, the war in Europe and the war in the Pacific. My crawling and toddling years were spent on living room and kitchen floors looking up legs of preoccupied adults for the duration in a world gone mad—a world at war with things so turned upside down and people so frightened, nobody at home bothered to make a point of telling me that one not-so-insignificant little detail—that the place my mother and father bought three years before I was born and where we would move to after the war; the place that waited for us in the country—was once a county park our father and mother bought in 1938.

Who buys county parks?

My parents had to have been money rich to be able to buy a public park (Delphi Falls) during a world depression.

Until I was 15, I was clueless to that reality. Growing up, it never dawned on me we might be rich just because we had four sofas and a bunch of chairs in the living room. I just figured the room, once an old dance pavilion, was so big it'd look stupid with one sofa.

By the time we moved to Delphi Falls, my older brothers and sisters were away from home, at college, or married with children, and the family's historical rumors and anecdotes had gone with them. I've since learned that if we were a typical family of eight children, the first four got raised as children with blazers, private music lessons, and tutors. The second four of us got raised like grandchildren.

Chapter 8

"Where's Korea, Dad?" ~ Jerome Mark Antil

Until the bottom eventually dropped out—or better-put, the rug got pulled out from under my father, my time with him had been rich *us* time, rich *together* time. I remember when our bond began. It was during the war, when we lived in Cortland, before my First Communion. It started one day in the early 1940s. I was alone in our backyard on Helen Avenue, watching a dog chase a squirrel. The ground began to rumble and shake, and thundering roars filled the air with frightening timpani. I froze in fear, not knowing what was happening. There was no television throughout the war. We only got to watch the war on newsreels at the Saturday picture show when they'd show bombs exploding, tanks firing their cannons at buildings, and battleships exploding and sinking.

There I was, standing alone in the backyard in the early 1940s when the ground began shaking and a deafening concussion of noises rattled my imagination. The sky turned dark. There were hundreds of bombers flying over, flying so low they almost touched the treetops. I screamed at the top of my lungs while pissing myself. My sister saw me through a window and was frightened. She called my father at the bakery. He rushed home, carried me into the house and told me not to be afraid.

"Those are our boys, son. They're American planes, flying over Cortland on their way to Long Island, where they'll fill up with gasoline and fly to England so they can bomb Hitler," my father said.

That made me feel better for sure, and it bonded my father and me. We became inseparable. After that episode he took me everywhere. He'd take me on road trips to see grocery stores throughout the state. We drove through the Pine Camp, the military base in upstate New York, with soldiers saluting us. His bakery made their pies and cakes. As we'd drive through the fort, I'd see German prisoners of war with POW printed on the backs of their coveralls standing behind barbed wire fences. One day my father told me why I was special to him. He said it was because I watched and listened, and that's how I learned. He'd say when someone knows how to do that—watch and listen—they learn more than those who talk, talk, talk and never listen. He told me his mother taught him how to listen and learn even without his going on to school past the ninth grade.

"Are you smart, Dad?" I asked.

"I can do a *Times* crossword in minutes, son."

"Dad, why did those bombers look like they were going to drop bombs?" I asked.

"You mean, why were they flying so low?"

"Yes."

"Son, with the war on, there are spies everywhere— enemy spies. If those planes flew high in the sky, an enemy spy could count the number of bombers or fighter planes and they could tell Hitler's army how many of our planes are on their way over to bomb him. When they fly low like they did over you, son, that's what they call bush hopping—flying low, just above the trees. They bush hop so they can't be counted by spies."

I remember that talk—every word—and understanding it as if it had happened yesterday. Kids grew up fast in the early 1940s. We had to. I don't know how old I was at the time of the bomber flyover, but it was for certain the war in Europe was still raging. VE Day wouldn't happen until I was four.

Every time my father asked me to jump in the car, I knew we'd be on an adventure, and I'd learn something.

We were settled in Delphi Falls before the Korean conflict started in 1950. Hearing about another war scared me. I didn't know where Korea was. I climbed the side hill up to the big white rock that jutted out near the top of the cliff. I would sit on the white rock to think, high above the house below. I remember watching my father driving in and parking behind the swing set. Walking to the house, he looked up, saw me on the white rock, and waved for me to come down. My father knew me pretty well. He knew I probably had something on my mind, sitting up there alone.

He was pouring coffee in the kitchen. I asked him about the Korean War and some questions about what the Cold War was, and were we going to get bombed? He told me he was thinking about building a bomb shelter on the side of the house to keep us safe, and maybe I could help build it. I asked him if the planes I could see flying over were enemy bombers. My father set his coffee on the counter and pointed his finger to tell me to wait there. He excused himself, went into his and my mother's bedroom and made a telephone call. When he came out, he told me he was taking me on an adventure in the morning. He told me to get a good night's sleep and maybe we could get some fishing in too, at Little York Lake.

Early the next morning, a Saturday, my father drove us forty-seven miles to the Tompkins Airport in Ithaca, NY. It was the first time I had ever seen an airport. I saw several small planes, and near a terminal gate there was a DC-3, an American Airlines twin engine propellor passenger airplane.

My father parked the car and we got out. He told me to stay by the car, he would be right back. He came out of the terminal and walked over to where I was standing and handed me an airline ticket.

"What's this?" I asked.

"It's a ticket for this plane. It's headed to Syracuse. Get on it, son."

"What do you mean, Dad?"

"Get on the plane, son."

"Are you going too, Dad?"

My father knelt on one knee and looked me in the eyes. He told me that it was going to be my big adventure, flying in an airplane. After that, I'd never be afraid of airplanes again.

The stewardess welcomed me to climb up the side ladder into the plane, and the captain invited me to sit beside him and let me hold the steering wheel. Except for the stewardess and the captain and copilot, I was the only passenger on the plane. I remember looking at my ticket and then looking out through the window as we taxied, and being pushed back into my seat as we took off and left the ground.

I remember the majesty of the flight—as if I could see a whole new world—a world not to be afraid of anymore, airplanes included. When we landed in Syracuse, I stepped out of the airplane with confidence. My father was at the gate waving at me. He had driven from Thompkins Airport to Syracuse's Hancock Field and had beaten the plane. That plane ride was a thrill of my lifetime. I will never forget it. I learned later that my father had purchased every ticket for that flight so I wouldn't be distracted from my big adventure.

Chapter 9

"What's My Line?" ~ CBS

1951 was a time of television's infancy in rural communities. If a neighbor's chimney had a proper antenna attached, they might have picked up two local channels that would shut down at midnight after a full orchestra's "The Star-Spangled Banner" and then to a snowy screen with a nerve-racking monotone hum until the dawn of a new day. In the early days of television, it was mostly programming for parents—news or intellectual game panel shows.

With television, the Cold War became the news, and I'd go to bed at ten, wondering if the world was about to explode. Would hydrogen bombs drop from Russia, making us communists? Every week, air raid sirens near the school would ring out ear-deafening blares, and the teachers would order us to crawl under our desks and to hold our hands over our eyes to keep from being blinded by the flash.

My first time under my school desk, not knowing what to expect, thinking back to when I was four, in Cortland during the war—being at the shoeshine parlor on Main Street with my father. I wasn't talking then, but I was a good listener, and while my father got his shine, he read the morning newspaper about the war. He and another man spoke about Europe and the Pacific, and my father said, "Nobody ever made a weapon to wound people, they only make weapons to kill." Then he added, "Best not to egg on or get egged into a fight. Best to walk away if you can, but if you can't walk away—make damn sure you win."

Thinking back, I knew his *win* was a metaphor for *kill*.

Once, during an air raid siren, I remembered how frightened we were after Japan bombed Pearl Harbor, how the emperor of Japan refused to end the war in the Pacific even after President Truman's threat of "prompt and utter destruction" and I'd think of my father's advice about walking away if you can. It came back to me on a school bus ride. I'd get tears thinking how our atom bombs killed or wounded hundreds of thousands of innocent civilians in Japan in a matter of a few seconds. I still pause at the thought.

At Delphi Falls, a brother tripped and fell in the living room. His mouth hit the fireplace brick and his two front teeth got mashed together. He was afraid of dentists, and my mother didn't force him to go to one right away. I felt sorry for him when it happened, and for his being afraid of a dentist, but I never considered teasing him about his front teeth until the day I got up late after having wet the bed. I took a shower and raced out to the school bus, thanked Ralph, the driver, for waiting, jumped on and sat down. That brother was sitting across the aisle, two rows back, looking pissed because the bus driver had waited for me like I was some kind of a prima donna.

He looked at me with a sneer and just enough so I could read his lips, he mouthed, "Wetter-bed!" Then he grinned.

He thought it was funny. Maybe it was, but at the time I thought of what my father said about fighting—and thinking this was the first time anyone called me that word and maybe it would only be round one of a constant fight if I let it slide. Maybe not that morning on the school bus, but maybe if I walked away he'd call me it again in a week or in a month. So, I fired back.

"Slop chops," I whispered.

His face bolted—almost to tears, but he never made fun of my bed-wetting again. I turned forward in my bus seat, feeling bad about saying it to him, but I felt good about the *kill*. Walking to the house from the bus later that day, we apologized to each other. He eventually got braces.

Chapter 10

"Summer 1952—Rock-a-bye-Baby." ~ Mother Goose

I was pretty much like any eleven-year-old kid, at an age we'd think we were invincible and that our guardians—or our mothers and fathers—would always be there for us.

It was June. When the teacher opened a classroom window, the smell of spring and fresh-mowed clover outside filled the room. School was about to let out for the summer and my mother announced at the dinner table that she was going to take Dick (16), Jim (8), Paul (13), and me (11) on a three-week road trip vacation. She announced we were going to drive and visit relatives we hadn't seen since our move to Delphi Falls from Cortland—and some we've never met. We were going to visit states none of us had been to before—Minnesota, where my mother and father grew up, and Arkansas, where my sister and her husband lived, and the states in between.

My mother's mother and father (Boma and Bompa) lived in Buffalo Lake, Minnesota. My father's six brothers lived near that lake. Mother's plan was that after we drove to Minnesota and visited, we would drive down to Little Rock, Arkansas, to see our sister, Mary. Mary was about to have another baby. My father couldn't take the time away from the bakery to make the long drive with us, but he would fly down and meet us in Little

Rock after the baby came and then fly back home to work.

As we drove off, Dick and Mother sat in the front seat. Mother drove most of the way to Minnesota, but Dick had his learner's permit and was able to help drive in daylight hours. Jim, Paul, and I were in the back seat. Every night we'd stop at tourist cabins and rent a cabin for the night.

Driving into Minnesota was like being in another country. Seeing wooded areas with lake after lake was almost like we were driving back in time. It took three days to get from Delphi Falls to Bompa Fred and Boma Jo's house. Their place was remote and on a lake, but with 10,000 lakes, every place in Minnesota was remote. We turned onto a road and drove past an impressive Catholic seminary campus. Mother told us guys went there to become priests. I remember passing the seminary and coming onto a cinder gravel drive. It was almost like we were driving through a time tunnel.

When our car stopped, we were at an empty, one-car garage with asphalt shingled siding with its doors pulled open wide. There was no car nearby, so we parked in front of it. The garage's inside looked like a craftsman's woodworking shop. It had a workbench with a half-built birdhouse on it and stuff like a vice grip holding a model airplane missing a propeller. There was a small table saw, a wood plane, and stacks of cut wood.

Boma and Bompa's place was like a summer camp with two or three acres of lawn on a slightly slanted hill by the lake. At the upper level off in a corner of the property was a *necessary,* an outhouse. It was a wood shanty, and on its front door was a carved-out crescent of a moon.

The main house was one story, and it had electricity. The entire property was once their family summer camp, but in their late years, Boma and Bompa moved to it year-round and sold their town home in the village of Maple Lake. Off to one side by the tree line was a dormitory with five sets of bunk beds for summer guests. The dormitory was rarely used anymore, but Dick, Paul, Jim, and I were going to sleep in it on bunk beds.

The main house was small, shaped like a compact letter T. On its outside left front corner was an oak rain barrel with a cloth covering it, a string holding the cloth tight to the rim of the barrel. When rain splashed into it, Boma Jo would use the rain-soft water to wash her hair. The main house had a small dining room, a living room with a floor model radio, and two bedrooms. The hallway could double as a sleeping porch with fold-up beds rolled against the walls, covered with blankets. There was a potty chair in the center area. My curiosity studied it but I never asked about it. The chair had a wide wooden lid on its seat, like a toilet seat lid because that's what it was, but with no plumbing. Under the lid rested a crockery pot.

The kitchen wasn't in the house. There was a flat stone walk from the front door about ten feet out to a separate, two-room kitchen house they called the cook shack. It was a screened-in shack with a large, wood-burning Franklin stove with iron stove tops and ovens. There was a sheet tin sink built into a wooden shelf with a hand pump for pulling water from a well. There were cabinets lining the walls, some filled with dishware, pots, pans, and shelves with Mason jars with paper labeled preserves in them. A wood table in the center of the room had a rolling pin on it and a meat grinder attached to it. There were pots and pans hanging below it.

The second room in the cook shack was used by Boma and Bompa as a morning "freshening up" room. It had a mirror, a large bowl, and a water pitcher for shaving or stand-up baths. To the side of the cook house was a lean-to door that led down to a small underground root cellar. They stored fruits and vegetables there because below-the-surface Earth temperatures don't vary much with seasons, or so Bompa told us. Bompa also told me the cook shack was separate from the house, so if there was ever a fire in it, the main house wouldn't catch fire as well.

As old as Bompa Fred and Boma Jo were, I had a sense that everything they did and how they did it had a purpose. How they lived made sense. It didn't take long to get used to walking up the back hill and going to the outhouse. It had two potty holes on a worn-smooth wooden bench in it, and it didn't stink like I thought it would.

Bompa Fred gave us a talk before we used it first time.

"A gentleman going in the outside convenience will always do his business sitting down, boys."

"No one wants to sit on a wet seat," Boma Jo said.

For toilet paper there were two options. For the men, there was a rope stretched with a mail-order catalogue with newsprint pages hanging on it. When you needed to wipe, you'd pull a page from the catalog and use that and drop it down the hole you were sitting on. For the ladies, there was a roll of tissue paper on a shelf in the house the ladies could carry up with them.

It was fun learning this way of life. I'd seen outhouses around Delphi Falls, but I'd never used one. Bompa Fred taught me lots of good stuff, like never swat at a wasp or a bee. It only ticks them off. He said wasps and bees would mind their business and let you do your business.

One day Mother came outside in a bathing suit. None of us kids had ever seen our mother in a bathing suit before. She was smiling like she was a little girl again and all of us, including Bompa Fred, climbed the steep wooden steps down from the house to the lake and jumped in. It was fun dog- paddling and swimming under water. Bompa Fred could float on his back, looking like he was napping. My mother, once a professional speed swimmer, was telling us we should learn the crawl—a swimming stroke we'd need if we ever wanted to be champion swimmers or lifeguards. Mother impressed us with her speed, demonstrating the long, high arm lifts and deep-water strokes, when her swimsuit top came down and a breast was bare during three strokes. Mother paid it no mind. She pulled her strap back up and kept swimming like she was a kid again. Later, behind the garage, my brothers and I were giggling about Mother's boob busting out of her swimsuit when Dick told us to shut up. He set us straight, reminding us our mother was a mother of eight and that we didn't see anything on the lake we hadn't seen before from the time we were firstborns. Dick was young but he was tall, and he looked down at us with a scowl on his face as if he was scolding us. Paul, Jim, and I started feeling guilty before Dick broke the moment.

"I think she was doing a breaststroke, not a crawl," Dick said.

It was at that moment behind the garage we knew the trip to Minnesota was going to be fun. Dick pulled a pack of Pall Mall cigarettes from his pocket, flicked a stick match against the garage door, and lit one.

"Tell anybody I'm smokin', I'll dump you headfirst in the shithouse, got it?"

We promised to keep our mouths shut.

"And if you're gonna be pulling your puds, do it in the outhouse. Don't be pulling them on a bunk near mine."

Paul blushed. Young Jimmy and I shrugged our shoulders, neither of us having a clue as to what Dick was talking about.

Buffalo Lake, Minnesota, was a study in America's frontier past. I learned things about my mother and my father and the times when they grew up and where they grew up.

We left feeling good about our visit and our heritage, and we headed south. The drive to Little Rock was a whole different experience. It was scary for me, a dumb-ass kid. Not only was the car getting hotter than Hades, even with the windows open, but Dick would go out of his way to scare the crap out of me by telling us stories about our going south and the further south we went the hotter it would get because we were heading into the deep south and deep south southerners hated the Yankees, and we'd better watch out when we got there and try not to get shot or strung up in a tree.

When we finally got to my sister's house on Battery Street, I almost didn't want to get out of the car. I decided for sure to stay pretty close to home and keep my mouth shut because of Dick's warnings.

The house was a duplex. It had a downstairs apartment where my sister and her husband lived and an upstairs apartment. The upstairs was empty, so my sister's landlord let Paul and me sleep up there on canvas cots. Mother told Paul to keep waking me up so I wouldn't wet the bed. I was more scared of getting shot and strung up than I was about wetting the bed.

There was an alley behind this house. I made a friend who lived next door and spoke with a funny accent. I'd meet him in the alley and we'd play Pitch with his deck of playing cards. He pronounced *eight* as *eye't,* and it took me forever to figure out what he was saying most of the time, but we became friends. The worst time for me in Little Rock was when my mother put my little brother and me on a bus alone to the zoo. She told us to tell the bus driver we wanted to get off at the zoo and after we were finished seeing the zoo, we were to look both ways, cross the street, and catch the same bus coming back up Battery Street toward home.

"Just tell the driver you want to get off at the stop when you can see our gray Chevrolet car in the driveway," my mother said.

We had fun at the zoo, but we spent our dimes on peanuts and didn't have bus money to go home. Jimmy had to pee and while he went, I sat on a curb in tears, afraid somebody would know I was a Yankee. A man came over and asked why I was crying, and I told him we forgot we needed bus money to go home to my sister's house and that we spent our money on peanuts.

The man was nice. He gave me enough for us to get on the bus and said, "This ought to get you home, son."

Standing up, wiping my eyes, I thanked him. I remember thinking that southern people don't hate Yankees. It was the days before most homes had television and before there was national news, and I was unaware of racial bigotry. I remember drinking from a water fountain at the zoo with a sign over it that read *COLORED* and thinking the water would have a special color of water come out, like lemonade. I started to tell the story about the colored water at the dinner table and Dick interrupted me and told how he wasn't allowed to sit in the balcony at the movie house because that was for colored only. When I asked what that meant, my mother said she would explain it when we got back home. She told Dick to button it, meaning "Shut up!"

On left, Mother sitting and Father standing.

Dick, Mike, Fred, Dorothy, Mary, Paul, me, Jim

My sister had her baby. The worst thing for me about the trip to Little Rock was that I took six rolls of pictures with my Brownie camera and I left them in one of the motel cabins on our way home. By the time I thought of them, my mother wouldn't turn around and drive back to get them. I remember the miserable heat in the car most of the way home.

Chapter 11

"When the Bough Breaks..." ~ *Nursery Rhyme*

My first reality wakeup call was about to happen—my life's first curve ball, low and outside.

I was trying to make sense of everything I had witnessed on our road trip. I was beginning to understand that America was bigger and more diverse than our safety nest between two cliffs and the Delphi Falls. I had seen how my grandparents survived by living happy, simple lives in Minnesota. They lived with nature by respecting it, learning from it and adapting to it. In Little Rock, I had my first taste of racism and of people hatred, passing through villages on country roads and watching how people lived. Sometimes we'd see abandoned slave quarters.

Everything I experienced on the trip to Minnesota and to Arkansas would churn in my mind for years. I don't remember how long it took us to get back to Delphi Falls from Arkansas—three, maybe four days—but it was hotter than blazes sitting in the back seat of an unairconditioned car with two brothers often making their points by punching each other's arms.

My father was home; his car was there. My mother asked Dick to park behind the swings near the flagpole. She told us she was going to surprise our father and wanted to go in ahead of us to give him a big hug.

When my brothers and I got inside, the shit hit the fan.

THE BOY AND THE BIG WHITE ROCK

To understand what went down, you've got to know our living room was this big room that used to be part of a pavilion—part of a dance hall. It was so big it had several couches, a piano against the wall and a bunch of chairs in it. There were large picture windows with shutters from when it was a dance pavilion. The rest of the old dance hall was now bedrooms, bathrooms, a kitchen, and dining room. There was also a laundry room.

When we left to go on this three-week road vacation the living room had a linoleum tile floor with some area rugs on it. Now, all of a sudden, that same floor was newly carpeted with a kind of lime green wall-to-wall carpeting. The next thing were the windows. When we left on our vacation, there were seven four-by-eight-feet windows with no curtains. We could stand in the living room and see the cliffs, the woods, and the waterfalls.

We'd come home to find the living room windows now had new draperies hanging on rods and pulled closed. Next to a turned-on lamp by the sofa where my father was standing with a grin was a new mink coat for my mother. He thought he was a hero, like he wanted it all—the carpet, the drapes, the mink coat—to be a surprise for our mother, but I'll be damned if she didn't have a mean look in her eyes, one I had never seen before. She stood tall, and my mother was six-feet-tall, so she could stand tall, and that's when she blurted out the following.

"Get me some money, Mike—lots of it. I'm leaving."

We thought she was fooling.

"Jerry, Jimmy, get in the car," my mother said.

"What!?" I asked.

"Now!" she growled.

We went to the car and got in the back seat. Mother came outside, climbed in and without saying a word, she drove eighteen miles to Syracuse, stopped and parked in front of a *Room for Rent* sign on the lawn of a turn-of-the-century, four-story house on Salina Street. She told us to wait in the car as she went in and rented a room.

For two days my mother never said a word—just sat and looked out the window. I can remember like it was yesterday, staring down at the street below and imagining every car passing as if they were passing through the rest of my life, then and forever unimportant. I felt as if I didn't matter anymore. For two days I never stopped crying—I'm talking twenty-four hours a day and as loud as I could. And for those two days I dumped my plates of food into the waste basket.

Mother finally took us home, and the day after we got home it was like nothing had happened between her and my father. Turned out my mother was jealous that she didn't get to pick out the carpet, the drapes, and the fur coat. (My father's secretary picked them out.) He only wanted to be my mother's hero and surprise her. He just pissed her off having his secretary do it. They put it behind them, but that episode was the reason there was a $6,000 mortgage put on the Delphi Falls property for the first time. It was my mother's "mad money."

By telling you about that incident I meant no disrespect to my folks. Talking about it, about how I felt that they weren't there for me (or my brother Jim) at the time and my brother and me having to spend the two days in a Syracuse rooming house. It was the moment my self-confidence was first shaken.

After it was over I always felt lonely. Not an alone lonely, but an *I'd always be on my own* kind of lonely. Moving forward I had a sense from that time I spent in a rooming house there'd be mountains in life I'd have to climb with no help. I did believe I could survive by not looking back or down but only looking forward.

It was like, who could I trust?

Chapter 12

1953 – "So far, this is the oldest I've been." ~ George Carlin

I remember thinking at the time, 12-year-olds like me had things going on that were crazy. Things happening nobody warned me about—body part things being some of them. Another big one was I had to start to get ready for manhood. My Holy Confirmation was coming up the following year, when I'd turn 13. The ceremony would be at St. Anne's in Manlius.

In the Catholic church a confirmation is a big deal—the Catholic counterpart of a Jewish bar mitzvah—but in the Catholic church it's for boys and girls. Father Lynch told us how important confirmation was, and he suggested we take the year to reflect on it and think about what kind of men and women we wanted to be. A real bishop would be there to bless our foreheads with holy oil, and there'd be a whole Solemn High Mass thing—the works. It'd be kind of like my first Holy Communion because it's a sacrament. But after Father Lynch explained how big a deal confirmation was, I promised myself I wouldn't screw up the ceremony like I did my First Communion, like the time I went into the confessional for the first time and couldn't think of a damn sin to confess. What five-year-old sins, for Christ's sake? I remember when I was four having to kneel in front of dead people in the funeral home next to St. Mary's Catholic School being less intimidating than my first confession for my First Communion.

There I was—first grade—in my first pair of long pants in a scary dark confessional, knees kneeling on a creaky wooden step I could hardly balance on, trying to look over the bottom of a screen door with a bored priest sitting behind it, staring like a ghost. I made up some bullshit sin—"I stole a pencil."

I had a year to get ready for my confirmation, and I decided not to take chances on screwing it up, of looking like a doofus again. I promised myself I was going to read the Bible, just in case somebody asked if I had. I'd get in bed and read portions of it every night and I've got to tell you. I liked it. I found this Jesus guy a cool dude. He was the kind of guy you'd like to have as a brother or an uncle—something like that.

I can also remember, when I was 12, sensing my father was changing somehow. He seemed more introspective, more to himself, detached. He hadn't been the same since his bakery partner died. Roy Parks, a newspaper magnate owned hundreds of newspapers. Duncan Hines was a nationally travelled salesman who was famous for recommending restaurants to the public and wanted to brand his well-known name on a consumer product. He had failed on several attempts. Duncan Hines then went to Roy Parks to ask for help. Roy Parks told him my father was the brightest marketing innovator he knew. My father and his bakery in Homer created and launched Duncan Hines bread—the baking brand later to be sold to Proctor and Gamble.

My father introducing Duncan Hines brand.

Following that, Walt Disney—the creator of Mickey Mouse—called my father at our home in Delphi Falls and asked my father if he could create a Disney-oriented loaf of bread. The Disney company would earn a penny a loaf for use of the Disney character brand. Walt Disney had the number one rated television show on the air called Davy Crocket and he was famous worldwide for the full feature Disney cartoons, Cinderella, Snow White and the Seven Dwarfs and Pinocchio. The bakery created Donald Duck Bread for Walt Disney and the first loaves were baked in my father's Carthage bakery.

Throughout this pressure, my father had been hospitalized twice, once for stomach surgery to remove an ulcer and once because he took a fall from a ladder and broke his leg in two places. I was standing ten feet away when the ladder came down. I watched a rung of the ladder snap his calf like a twig. My father just lay on the ground, with everyone screaming. Chills went up my spine.

On the day he got the cast removed he asked me to get in the car.

"Where we going, Dad?" I asked.

"We have a couple of stops to make, son, but we'll stay at the Imperial Hotel in Carthage tonight."

"Room six, Dad?" I asked.

"Room number six, son," he said.

My father would always get Room Number Six on the hotel's second floor because it had a balcony, and he said if the hotel ever caught on fire, we could get out and shimmy down from the balcony. My mother handed me a sack with my toothbrush and underwear in it. It was a quiet ride, and I respected my father's silence. I knew he had a lot on his mind. We drove to Syracuse and eventually pulled into a radio station's parking lot.

"C'mon in, son," my father said.

We went in the building and my father opened a door into a recording studio. A man was playing a piano, and a radio announcer was doing vocal exercises into a microphone. My father pointed at a chair by the wall for me to sit and wait. For the next half hour the man at the piano would play music and the announcer would read a radio commercial about Donald Duck Bread. When they finished, my father and I left the studio. In the car, I turned to my father.

"Dad, how come they didn't play Disney music?"

My father turned and looked at me with a wince.

"What do you mean, son?"

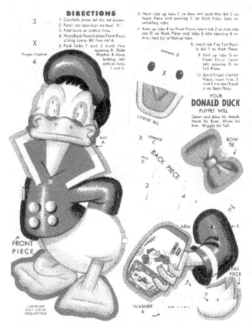

Donald Duck Bread

"They were talking about Donald Duck Bread, Dad, but that man was playing *froufrou* music on the piano."

"What should they have played, son?"

"How about, 'Hi ho, hi ho, it's off to work we go,'—or what about, 'Some Day My Prince Will Come'?"

My father pulled the keys from the ignition.

"Let's go back in, son," he said.

Inside the studio, my father told them my idea. Three people came over and shook my hand and congratulated me.

"Great idea, son," they offered. They re-recorded the commercials for Donald Duck Bread using Walt Disney music and they gave me credit for it.

My father was all smiles in the car. After driving a couple of hours into an area I wasn't familiar with, he turned on a dirt road into a sprawling field I had never seen before.

"Have you given much thought to what you want to be when you grow up, son?" my father asked.

"I don't know—maybe an architect," I said. "I don't know."

We were driving through a field filled with tall wheat shafts, without seeds on top.

"What is that?" I asked.

"In the field?" my father asked.

"Yes."

"It used to be wheat, son."

"If it used to be wheat, isn't it still wheat?"

"Wheat has a head, kernels. A reaper takes the kernels off to be milled into flour."

"I knew that."

"See the stalks?" my father asked.

"Yes."

"Know what they're called?"

"Stalks?"

"The shafts, son, they call that straw," my father said.

"Is that where straw comes from, Dad?"

"That's where straw comes from, son. Wheat stalks have no nutritional value, but they make good bedding for cows and horses."

I smiled at the wealth of knowledge my father had. My smiles were that he would go out of his way to share it. And he was the kind of a man who would go out of his way to give a 12-year-old kid the credit for dreaming up the best Donald Duck radio commercials—a moment that would affect my life and confidence forever.

We came to a curving dirt road that entered thick walls of junglelike, tall, moss-covered trees.

"Where're we going, Dad?"

"It's a surprise, son."

Northern forests in New York were ageless, untamed, thick growths of trees, vines and moss—a semi-wilderness. Our car eventually came to a cabin on the bank of a dark, very wide river.

"Where are we?" I asked.

"That's the Black River, son."

He pulled to a stop in front of a cabin door. The cabin was shingled on its sides with a powdery gray cedar shake and it had a green, moss-covered shake roof. The river behind it was dark, wide, and foreboding.

"Why's everything so dark, Dad?"

"Trees are pretty thick, son. Keeps the light out."

"No, I mean the river—it's pitch black."
"Mineral deposits, son."
"It's scary," I said.
"It flows north," my father said.
"I didn't know a river could flow north," I said.
"Heard of the Nile, son?"
"The Nile River in Egypt? Sure."
"The Nile flows north, son—many rivers flow north."
"I didn't know that."
"Pine Camp (Fort Drum) isn't far away."
"What are we doing here, Dad?"
"I need to get something."
My father pointed at a small boat tied to the pier. "That."
"That boat?"
"That's not just a boat, son…that's a whaler. Ever heard of a Boston whaler?"
"No."
"Let's get out and take a look."
"Did you buy it, Dad?"
"It's a small Boston Whaler. It belongs to a friend of mine who works in the Carthage bakery. He told me if I could manage to get his boat to Carthage, he'd sell me the motor, cheap. He doesn't have a trailer, but he wants to keep the boat in Carthage."
"What could we do with a boat motor, Dad?"
"Ain't it a pip, son?"
"We don't have a boat, Dad."

"Remember the time you and I were in the rowboat we rented and we were fishing on Oneida Lake?"

"Which time?"

"The time the heavy rains came over the lake and almost sank us before I could row us to shore?"

"I thought we were goners for sure," I said.

"Well, son, we could use that motor on Oneida Lake when we go fishing there—just in case of rain."

"How are we getting the boat to Carthage without a trailer, Dad?"

"Carthage is north, son, and it's on this Black River," he said.

"How far away?" I asked.

"Not far—half a dozen miles maybe."

I liked the boat's look with its oars and motor. The front of it was taller than the back end. My father explained that was so it could break through tall, crashing, sea waves.

"We'll fill the tank and a spare can of gas, son."

"Who will give us a ride back to get the car, Dad?"

"Son, I need you to drive the boat up to Carthage."

"What?"

"I'll meet you up there, son."

"Huh?"

"Simple. When you come into Carthage, you'll see the big bridge. Just pull it up on the bank under the silver steel bridge, son. You can't miss it."

I stared at my father.

"You can do it, son."
"Me drive it alone? I've never—"
"You camp out alone, right?"
"Yeh, but—"
"It's like camping, son. Nothing to be afraid of."
"But I've never run a boat motor, Dad."
"Nothing to it. Hop in, check it out."

My father took a broom resting on a tinder box and handed it to me.

"Clear the leaves out, son. I'll find a gas can."

I was still feeling good about helping my father make radio commercials and being treated like an adult. Now for the first time I felt like I was about to help my father out without being selfish and asking him my usual lot of questions. It was because of the quiet ride we had in the car. That ride was when I saw a different side of him for the first time—a noticeably disengaged, distracted side. I respected and loved my father too much to interrupt his thoughts with dumb questions. I cleared the leaves from the boat and handed him the broom. He put it in the woodshed and handed me a gas can and a paper sack.

"Here's some sandwiches, son."

I set the sack on the seat in the middle of the whaler.

"Pull the throttle, then pull on the starter rope," my father said. "Be patient, son. It takes long, fast pulls. It doesn't always start on one pull. Just keep pulling until it starts. You'll get the hang of it."

"What do I do if it starts?"
"Once it starts push the throttle in."

"Then what?"

"See the black rubber grip on the handle, son?"

"Yes."

"That grip is the accelerator—it's like the motor's gas pedal. Hold that rubber grip, turn it to go up and down on speed and you move the rod back and forth—that steers the boat—one way right or the other way left. Understand, son?"

"I think so."

"To make the motor push the boat you turn the throttle, the rubber grip. Always keep your hand on that grip when the motor is running. The more you turn the grip the faster you'll go. Keep it slow until you get the feel of it—until you feel comfortable. You'll get the hang of it."

"Now what?" I asked.

"Watch out for floating logs. Go around them."

He pointed to the right.

"That way is north, son. Follow the river north until you come to the steel bridge in Carthage—you'll know it when you see it. You'll see my car parked on top. I'll be in the car, waiting."

"What if the engine stalls out or stops, and I can't get it started again, Dad?"

"It shouldn't, son. It's pretty reliable."

"But what if—?"

"If it does, don't panic. Just remember the river flows north. It'll float you all the way up to Carthage without doing anything. Just attach the oars and row it, like you row us out on Sandy Pond when we fish."

My boat ride alone up the Black River was a lifetime adventure memory—riding the keel of being listened to by professional adults in a radio recording studio. Not even a teenager and I inspired some Walt Disney radio commercials.

As the whaler navigated the river, it plowed a good wave in front. I saw wild game I'd never seen before—one young black bear, circling chicken hawks, one swooping down to grab a chipmunk for dinner, and turtles resting on the roots of trees for sun. In one horizon against a peeking sunset, I could see a silhouette of a bull moose.

Like Mark Twain's steamboat, I imagined my way through many miles before the bright, small bubbles of street lighting began to populate the horizon. I got within eyesight of the steel bridge and I breathed easier. I felt good about myself, like I had accomplished something.

I could see my father's car on top of the bridge. I turned a hard right and kept speed to run the boat onto the shore. I jumped out and tied it to a steel post. I climbed the bridge and walked to his car. My father's head was rested back. He was asleep. I tapped on the window. He woke from his nap, sat up and smiled. When he opened the car door a miasma of stale alcohol followed him out like a morning smell of sulfur in Delphi. I saw an empty liquor bottle on the seat next to where he was sitting. I pretended not to notice. He leaned back against the car. I didn't look at him.

"How was the ride, son?"

"It was great, Dad! It got me to thinking."

"How's that, son?"

"I was thinking maybe I'd like to be a forest ranger. What do you think?"

My father paused in thought.

"It doesn't matter what a person chooses to do in life—just be your best at it and you'll always make a good living. Be yourself—and be your best."

"So, I could be a ranger?"

"Give it some time, son. There are any number of things you could be."

"I'm not all that smart, Dad."

"You're only twelve and you've already produced radio commercials for Walt Disney, and you've navigated a dozen miles on the Black River and you say you're not smart?"

"I can hardly read a book."

"Then you need a different librarian, son. What kind of books are you reading?"

"No plots in algebra. General science books, Dad."

"Son, when you find an interest, you'll devour books about the subject."

"Really?"

"You must have given it some thought before your boat ride today, son, what started you thinking about being a forest ranger?"

"*Outdoor Life*, the magazine."

"Reading is reading, son. That's a book with a paper cover."

I turned around and looked at my father. I had a feeling inside me like maybe I was becoming a man. There were tears in my father's eyes.

"What's wrong, Dad?"

"You remind me of my brother ... Hubert," my father said.

"Uncle Hubert. In Minnesota. I met him, Dad."

"Hubert died yesterday, son."

I clasped my mouth with my fingers.

"He passed in his sleep."

"He was a nice man. He looked like you, Dad."

"Too young to die," my father said. He wiped his eyes with his handkerchief. "I'm going up to bed. It'll be an early morning."

My father always had two mornings—his first morning was at 2:00 a.m. when bakeries came alive and trucks got loaded and the dough mixing, baking and wrapping changed shifts. My father would be there with his crews of bakers and route salesman. His second morning, if we were in Carthage, was to have breakfast with me before we left for home. He stepped away from the car and walked over to the bridge railing, leaned on it and looked down.

"Did you tie the boat up good, son? A tight knot?"

"It won't be going anywhere, Dad."

"Proud of you, son. Let's go. We'll look after it in the morning. I've got you the room attached to number 6. It connects."

He handed me his car keys, my room key, and a five-dollar bill.

"Son, I'm going to walk to the hotel. Park it somewhere for me."

"Okay, Dad."

"Grab a sandwich, something to eat, maybe get yourself a magazine, and I'll see you in the morning."

Imperial Hotel – Room Number 6

When I finally got to my room, I could hear coughing throughout the night. At first, I thought the sounds were his crying because his brother Hubert had died, but I fell asleep thinking it was a smoker's cough.

Chapter 13

1953- "Dream as if you'll live forever. Live as if you'll die today." ~ James Dean

My brother Dick was of an age and temperament when he and some of his buddies would always go out of their way to look for trouble. Late at night they were known to "borrow" their parents' cars (without their knowledge) and drag race at 100 mph-plus speeds from Hastings' corner store in Delphi down the Oran Delphi Road to Cherry Valley (Route 20), up the hill partway and then back.

Dick was going through a period of getting in trouble for fistfights, sometimes for inappropriate touching on the school bus. By the time he was 16, a general consensus was my brother would be the first in reform school or worse. All that aside, there was one thing certain. My father would never give up on anyone willing to make an effort and try to better themselves. One night at the dinner table, my father flat out fired a broadside over Dick's bow, catching the self-admitted no-account rabble rouser totally off guard.

"Dick, have you ever earned money by creating something from scratch or owning something? I'm not talking getting paid to wash dishes or to mow lawns, son. I'm talking having something of your own you managed?"

"You including poker? Horse track betting, Dad?" Dick snickered.

"Don't toy with me, son. If you don't want to hear me out, I'll find someone who does," my father said.

"Sorry, Dad—I'm listening," Dick replied.

"In Fayetteville, there's this swimming hole. It's open to the public summers from Memorial Day to Labor Day. It's called Snook's Pond."

"I never heard of it, Dad."

"I met Mr. Snook. He's the owner. Met him at a meeting in Manlius. Their home is on the road in front of the spring-fed waterhole they own. They let people swim. People drive up their drive and park on the lawn, pay to swim."

My father explained that Snook's Pond had a small refreshment stand next to the swimming area, and if Dick agreed to see that the dirt walking paths got raked twice a day, saw to it that debris and cigarette butts got picked up, Mr. Snook would let him run the refreshment stand like it was his own and keep the profits from hot dog or soft drink sales.

"I'll do it, Dad. When do I start?" Dick asked.

"Hold on a minute, son. Don't you think you'll be needing some help?"

"What's so tough about selling pop and hot dogs?"

"Slow down, son. There might be a couple dozen hot dogs that need to be cooked all at once—and while someone's cooking, who's going to be selling? How about pop bottles that have to be iced down? And someone has to keep the stock up while someone else will have to tractor supplies up from their garage," my father said. "Don't forget raking the paths and picking up papers and cigarette butts goes with the deal."

Dick looked around the table for helpers.

"Paul?" Dick asked.

Paul wasn't interested. He was in love with a girl in Delphi and didn't want to leave for the summer.

"Jim?" Dick asked.

Jimmy wasn't interested. He sold *GRIT* newspapers to area farmers and popsicles in Delphi from his cart throughout the summer.

"Jerry?" Dick asked.

"For how much?" I asked.

"What?!" Dick snarled.

"Sounds like a management/labor thing," my father said.

I loved my brother Dick—I had to—but he had a reputation for dealing off the bottom of a deck in card games on the school bus.

"For how much?" I repeated.

"Three bucks a day," Dick said.

"Don't say bucks, dear," my mother said.

"Three dollars?" I asked. "I make one-fifty at Maxwell's mowing their lawn and that only takes two hours. And you're talking all day for three dollars. No way."

"Can you see girls running around in swimsuits down at Maxwell's? I don't think so," Dick said.

"Don't be rude, son," Mother warned.

"Five dollars a day," I said.

"May I make a suggestion?" my father asked.

Dick nodded.

"Since you've never done this before, there is no way of predicting sales or inventory costs. What's say you consider offering Jerry two dollars a day, plus free food—plus an end of the summer tally of profits giving him 20 percent for hanging in with you?"

"I'd be okay with that," Dick said.

"Who's watching the money?" I asked.

"I'll handle the books," my mother said.

"Then I'd do it," I said.

"Dick, you okay drawing two dollars a day too?" my mother asked.

"Okay," Dick said.

Dick and I shook on it and the next morning my father drove us to Snook's Pond to meet Mr. Snook. There was an entrance sign by the driveway to the right of their red house. In the back, on the right, was a two-car garage with a tractor parked inside. Mr. Snook explained that we could use the garage for storage of soft drinks and supplies, and we could use the tractor to bring them up the hill to the snack stand.

On the left of the entrance was a shack selling admission tickets and renting out lockers and towels. That shack faced the long swimming area. The bottom of the pond was dirt and the pond continued out into a spring-fed natural lake. There was a floating dock near the back of the swimming area where a lifeguard sat. Across the swimming area from the snack shack was a women's locker room. On our side, next to our snack shack, were men's lockers.

Mr. Snook had his oldest daughter give Dick a personal tour of the area. He asked his younger daughter to show me the different paths that would need raking and trash picked up from them. She showed me where the tools and trash containers were. After our orientation, my father suggested what inventory we might start with, and where to call to order it. My mother opened a checking account and seeded it with startup money. She put some cash in the cash drawer.

"Bring the cash drawer home every day, Dick. I will handle your books," my mother said.

My father taught us how to cook and serve hot dogs in bulk, how to serve a soda pop, and how to try to upsell potato chips or Cracker Jack caramel popcorn.

In week one, Dick and I were dressed prim and proper. Long pants, shirt/collar, and all smiles. Week two we were in short shorts, smiles–upselling frozen Milky Way candy bars and lemonade along with hot dogs. By week three we were standing behind the counter in our swim trunks—Dick sneaking off during lulls to be with girls behind the men's locker room—and I found myself learning the art of kissing on occasion. I remember sometimes getting stiff while kissing, pretending it wasn't happening, almost as if it was a nuisance.

At summer's end, the pond closed on Labor Day weekend. It was abandoned with a feeling like it was never used. I went swimming for the last time.

A boy I recognized from Manlius walked through the swimming area grinning, taking delight in trashing the place. He'd kick over waste barrels with snarly guffaws and go out of his way to throw things about. I shouted at him to knock it off. He ran in my direction and jumped in the water with his clothes on and pushed me under. He put his feet on my neck and shoulders and held me down to a point I was certain I was going to gasp for air and drown if I did.

I struggled to push him off and managed to get above water to catch my breath. I can remember his smirk as I climbed out. I walked by him, shaking. I remember thinking if I had had a tool in my hand at the moment I walked by him, I would have killed him. I don't know what made me not go get a tool, but I didn't. I walked away and hitchhiked home in my swimsuit to Delphi Falls.

I opened this 12-year-old odyssey telling you there were a couple of things going on with me. I could have just blurted it out first that I was clueless about girls, sex, erections, and how babies were made and all that crap—those were big things. But being 12 for me was worse than being in the dark about any of that. I was a normal 11-year-old just one year before, but at 12 I'd turned into this string bean, six-foot-tall geek, still growing like a weed. I was skinny, looking like I was old enough to buy beer, dumber than rat bait about sex and worse, still wetting my bed. Kids called me beanpole. I was so clueless about procreation; one time my friend Johnny on the school bus was telling me things my sister who got married at the falls was doing with her husband on their honeymoon in Bermuda.

THE BOY AND THE BIG WHITE ROCK

My sister Dorothy's wedding reception at the Delphi Falls.

I got off the school bus at his stop at the bottom of the hill and told the bus driver he could take off—that I was going to walk home up over farmer Parker's hill in the back of Johnny's place. I waited until the bus drove away and then pushed Johnny back against a tree and threatened to pound him if he didn't take it back and admit it was all lies what he told me about my sister.

Johnny apologized.

"See ya' tomorrow," I said.

"See ya'," Johnny said.

I walked home.

It wasn't fun being six feet tall at 12 and still waking up in a wet bed; going to the bathroom, having to lean down to look in the mirror and seeing whitehead pimples on my face like I had caught the measles. As to the sex thing, my only hope was that I wasn't alone, and kids my age were going through it too, but were just afraid to talk about it. There was the one time this tall schoolmate (I barely knew him) invited me over for the first time to their farm on a Saturday. He told me they had a new tractor, and if I came over, he'd let me drive it. I'd never been to his farm, and I've got to tell you what happened just to show you how naïve I was at 12.

Up in his bedroom I was more embarrassed than curious when this stupid kid jumped out of his closet bare-ass naked, gripping an erection in his hand like it was a bamboo fishing pole. I remember the shit-eating grin on his face. I just shrugged my shoulders and turned away, telling him I'd meet him out by the tractor and walking out of the bedroom and going downstairs as if nothing had happened.

When I got home my brother Paul told me that the vacant farmhouse down the road from Mr. Petcavage's up above the second falls was on fire. It was a two-story farmhouse that had been abandoned during the Depression. Most of its windows had been broken by vandals throwing rocks, but it was still furnished—like a ghost house wanting to keep its memories alive. I went into Dick's room to ask if he heard about the fire and if he wanted to drive up to see it.

"Shut the door," Dick said.

I closed his door behind me.

"I set it," Dick said.

"What?!" I asked.

"Shut up!" Dick snarled. "Keep it down."

"Why'd you do it?" I asked. "You could get arrested if they find out."

"Me and a girl were doing it on the upstairs bed and when we got out of bed there was blood all over the blanket and mattress," Dick said.

I had no idea what he was telling me.

"You murdered a girl?" I asked.

"No, asshole. She got her period."

"What's a period?" I asked.

Dick looked at me. "You really don't know, do you?"

He turned to look out his window.

"They were going to tear it down anyway," Dick said.

"Is she dead?"

"She's fine. She's on the rag is all, I'm taking her to Suburban Park tonight."

I stared at him with a confused glare.

"You really don't have a clue what a girl's period means, do you?" Dick asked.

I stood there, dumbfounded.

"Tell anyone I set the fire and you've had it," Dick said. Until these few sentences, I've never breathed a word of my brother Dick's arson to a soul.

Getting ready for my confirmation, on every High Mass Sunday my mother would give me a choir robe from her closet for me to put on. It was like what a priest wears, but red. Parents had them made for their kids who sang in the choir. They kept them in their closets to keep them in one piece. Being in the choir, I got to stand near the altar, which was cool, but I had to be still. I envied altar boys in the black and white robes being able to move around, light the three candles on either side of the altar. Six candles signaled an hour-long High Mass. After they lit the candles, they'd genuflect before sitting and waiting for Father Lynch to come out, his arm outreached, swinging the smoking gold incense burner and walking the church aisles up and back, blessing the worshippers. You could hear the gold chain clanging on the burner.

I had a good feeling about God. I felt I could trust Him to keep secrets and because he could do miracles and anything He wanted, maybe He'd be there for me, like a magical friend. One night I rebooted my nighttime prayers. During the war my bedtime prayers were, *"…if I should die before I wake, I pray the Lord my soul to take."* Then, at 12, a long drink of water, pimply, a geek and being on what I thought was the good side of Jesus, my nightly prayer became a lot more specific. *"God, don't let me wet the bed tonight and God, please don't let me die with a hard-on."*

Chapter 14

"The best way to guarantee a loss is to quit." ~ Morgan Freeman

I was in the ninth grade, a high school freshman at 12. With my height I looked like a senior but, according to some bullshit athletic league rule, I was too young to play basketball—even Junior Varsity. Grade or girth had nothing to do with sports in the jungles of New York State—age did. If it weren't for my parents and my friends' parents, I would have been a bum.

On my first day, I was practicing loitering in the school hall at my locker when I looked up. She was a shadowed silhouette at first, but she soon resolved into the pretty face of a girl I had never seen before. There was a lost look in her eyes, as if she was approaching me to ask directions. She was tall and slender with curly brunette hair. She wore a pleated Irish plaid skirt and a Kelly green, front-buttoned sweater over a heavily starched white blouse with collar. She had a pretty, sparkling smile. It was infectious, and I could see a genuine, nonjudgmental happiness in her eyes.

"Hi," I said.

"Hello," she replied.

"I'm Jerry Antil."

"Hi, Jerry Antil. I'm Judy Sessions."

"First day, Judy Sessions?"

"My first day, Jerry Antil. I'm usually lost in Baltimore, and now I'm lost in Fabius. Go figure."

"You just move here?"

"Only temporarily. I'll be here while my parents are busy doing something."

"Oh."

"I'm living with my uncle," Judy said.

"Who's that?"

"Ted Dwyer."

"Oh."

"You know Ted Dwyer?"

"I know Ted," I said. "Everybody knows everybody here."

Ted Dwyer and his family lived in a small house at Gooseville Corner, just around the corner from where Jimmy Conway lived. Jimmy Conway was one of my brother Dick's best friends.

"Where's your locker?" I asked.

"I don't have one," Judy replied.

"You don't have a locker?"

"Not yet. I guess I go to the office for that."

"Whose homeroom are you in?"

When she told me her homeroom, I knew she was a sophomore—in the tenth grade.

"Use my locker," I said.

"Really?"

"Plenty of room."

"That's sweet."

"I never lock it."

"I don't need locks," Judy said.

She stacked books on the shelf and draped her sweater's label on a hook before closing the door.

She offered her hand.

"Thanks for sharing, Jerry. It's nice meeting

you." She smiled, turned, and walked away.

I was smitten on my first day of school as an underage freshman. I stood tall, like a sophomore or junior—like I was 15 instead of 12. I got to my homeroom and sat in the back to be alone and gather a strategy. My mission, for the next week at least, was to not do anything stupid that might give a hint of my age—not give any clue to Judy Sessions from Baltimore that I was a 12-year-old twerp. No girl had ever looked me in the eye like Judy Sessions had—not even the girl I kissed at Snook's Pond. To hell with basketball—that's for kids—I volunteered to be equipment manager for Coach Driscoll's football team. After all, the word *manager* had a more mature ring to it than *player*.

One small thing was about to pop up that could have jinxed my journey to love, Baltimore-style. Halloween was days away and my father announced at the dinner table that Clarence Nash was coming to our house for supper and that he might stay over.

"Who's Clarence Nash?" I asked.

"Clarence Nash, son, is a man who works for Walt Disney."

"Walt Disney, like the real Walt Disney?"

"The real Walt Disney, son."

"He does? What's he do for him?"

"Mr. Nash is the voice for the Walt Disney cartoon character, Donald Duck. There's going to be an on-stage presentation—a show—of Donald Duck Bread at a theater in Syracuse—Disney costumes, everything. Donald Duck will introduce Donald Duck Bread to the audience," my father said.

"Does this Mr. Nash know I helped with the radio commercials, Dad?"

"No, but he will, son," my father said. "The bakery will be handing out loaves of Donald Duck bread to everyone who comes for the show."

Clarence Nash arrived by train from California.

Clarence Nash did come to our house. He was a nice man. He told us that our father reminded him of

Walt Disney—they were both always creative and with positive, happy thoughts. He stood up at the table and demonstrated the voice he used when speaking as Donald Duck. He told us that in the show in Syracuse, Donald Duck was going to sing and squabble, and be a general nuisance while entertaining an audience of hundreds.

"Are you a ventriloquist?" my brother Dick asked.

"No, son. I'll stand behind the curtain with a microphone," Mr. Nash said. "Donald Duck will be in costume on stage, cavorting about, carrying on and entertaining. It'll be good fun."

My brother Jim told Mr. Nash about the Halloween costume parade that was going to be at school the following night. Jim mentioned it would be great if Donald Duck could be in the school's costume parade.

"When's your parade, son?" Mr. Nash asked.

"Tomorrow night," Jim said.

"Mike, I think we could arrange the loan of our Donald Duck costume for a school parade," Mr. Nash said.

"For real?" Jim asked.

"Clarence—" my father started. "Jerry here gave the radio guys the idea of using Disney music with the radio commercials. Perhaps Jerry could wear the Donald Duck costume?"

When my father said that, my mind started racing: *I just met this girl, Judy Sessions. She likes me. The last thing I want to do now is to parade around in a duck costume playing like a kid ... screwing up the ageless image she has of me.* I was about to pass on the whole idea of wearing the Donald Duck costume in the school parade until Mr. Nash set out the rules.

"With every Walt Disney character—and their costumes—there are some strict rules we have to adhere to," he said.

"Rules?" my father asked. "Listen up, Jerry."

"Rule one," Clarence Nash said. "At Disney, all of our Disney characters are real. No exceptions. No one will ever see anyone putting on a character's costume or taking off a character's costume, ever. When wearing a character's costume the wearer can never speak a word. No one is to know who's wearing the costume. It supports the illusion."

"It's like knowing magic is a trick, but enjoying the magic and not being told the trick," my brother Dick said.

"Couldn't have said it better," Clarence Nash replied. "The character will always and only be the character."

"And nobody would know who's inside?" I asked.

"Nobody will ever know who's inside," Clarance Nash said.

"Never, ever?" I asked.

"Never, ever," Clarence Nash repeated. "Mike, can one of your bread trucks deliver Jerry to the school in full costume—and bring him home in costume after?"

"Absolutely," my father said.

"No one can see me inside?" I asked.

"You can see out, no one can see in," Mr. Nash

said. "Donald's head is large enough to camouflage your height, Jerry. No one will ever know it's you inside."

The Halloween parade lasted four slow walks around the gymnasium at school. Donald Duck was a major hit. The good news was I passed by Judy Sessions four times. She loved the costume, howled at the fun of the party but never had a clue it was me inside. The next Monday she asked me why I wasn't at the Halloween parade. I told her I had to study. After saying that, I turned abruptly to go to my homeroom. I was a bad liar, and wouldn't hold a straight face had I stood there talking.

The first time Judy and I kissed was on the school bus after a roller-skating party at the Cortland roller rink. School buses were driving us from the rink back to the school, where parents would pick us up. After a test kiss or two—one prolonged kissing of her chin by mistake—Judy and I settled into liking to kiss and we genuinely liked being together. My brother Fred let me wear his high school ring so I'd look older. I wouldn't lie about whose it was if anyone were to ask, but no one ever asked. It made me feel subliminally older than 12.

At halftime of a football game, I was carrying a bucket of sliced oranges, handing them out to the players lying around, resting on the ground. One of the players stuck his foot out and tripped me. As I staggered, I swung around to catch my balance and my fist with my brother's ring on it struck his face. It required six stitches over his eye to patch him up. To this day I was never certain he was trying to trip me. I was not a violent guy, but my reputation for it was growing.

Chapter 15

"Life is just so PAINFUL and messy and HARD and WORTH IT and all that stuff." ~ Robert Downey, Jr.

We stepped off the school bus to a blanket of powdery snow covering like confectionary sugar a refrozen layer of melting crust. We had started walking the driveway when we first saw the car. It didn't belong to anyone we knew, and it began driving from the house down the snowy drive toward us. The snow crunched under its tires. We could tell by the stature of the silhouette that our father was in the back seat of the car—a passenger. A stranger was driving and a hospital nurse with a nurse's cap and navy-blue cape snapped around her neck was sitting on the passenger side of the front seat.

We stopped walking as the car approached so we could say hi to our father, but the car didn't stop. We bent down to look through the closed car windows as best we could in the glare of the sun. My father was waving, but the driver didn't slow down enough for us to make eye contact. The windows were closed, and the car kept moving with no regard for human emotion. It never slowed the entire distance to the front gate.

I speculated that he didn't open a window because it was cold. Maybe he wasn't feeling well. He'd been coughing a lot lately. Maybe they were taking him to the doctor to get some penicillin.

We watched our father turn around in the back seat and wave at us a gentle, sad wave. His eyes squinted from tears glistening in the sunlight. Our father was weeping, and we didn't know why or where they were taking him. We stood out of love and respect, just in case he was still watching us, until the car turned down Cardner Road. It picked up speed and drove out of sight.

He had never left us without saying goodbye. That wasn't how he was, and we had no idea why he was now. We ran into the house to find my mother standing in the book den, staring through the front window in tears.

"Where're they taking Dad?" my brother Dick asked.

"Why wouldn't he talk to us?" I asked.

"Why's Dad crying?" my brother Paul asked.

Without taking her eyes from the long driveway my mother told us to get out of our school clothes and meet her at the table. She made hot chocolate so we could sit and talk. After we changed, my mother had us come to the kitchen to get our cups and take them to the table. Now seeing us, she was smiling. I think it was because we were home and she wasn't alone. Jim was out delivering his newspaper and would be home soon. With the exception of that one two-day episode I told you about—my mother's jealous rage about the new drapes and carpet—my mother had not been separated from my father since the day they met and fell in love in 1919.

She sat tall at the table.

"Boys, I need you to be strong and to be my men of the house. We will get through this together," she said.

The phone started ringing. We let it ring.

"Your father and I chose not to tell you about what I am going to share until we were certain. We didn't want to worry you unnecessarily."

"What's wrong, Mom?" I asked.

"Tell us," Dick asked.

"Your father has tuberculosis. It's a bad disease."

"TB?" I asked.

"Yes, TB. They are taking him to the TB sanitarium. He will have to stay there until he gets better."

"Is that why he was coughing so much, Mom?" I asked.

"Yes, dear. Tuberculosis attacks the lungs, and it affects breathing."

I started to tear up.

"Is that why he couldn't stop and talk?" I asked.

"Oh no, son. Please don't think that. It's just that they don't know a lot about tuberculosis. They think it may be highly contagious in the early stages, like polio, but they're not sure. Once the people from the sanitarium came and told your father the test results confirmed he had TB, he couldn't risk exposing you. That's why he could only wave. He loves you so much—he would never not want to say goodbye to his children. Your father asked the driver to wait until the school bus came, so he could at least wave goodbye."

Our minds could get around this better, but the air was still tense. I couldn't grasp not being with my dad again.

"Can we go see him?" Dick asked.

My mother looked down at her hands. "I'm so sorry, boys, you can't—not until he's better—at least not until they know it's safe for you to see him. They have to confirm that he isn't contagious. Just pray for your father every day. Pray he'll come back healthy and strong."

"How long will he be gone?" I asked.

My mother looked at each of us.

"They told me it could be a year. It could be ..."

Knowing the statistics, that TB was the number one killer disease in America, my mother wept. She was a strong woman, but her face dropped into her hands in a despair we had never seen before. Dick jumped up and into her and my father's bedroom and came back with a handkerchief.

"Thank you, dear," she mumbled.

My mother looked at the tablecloth as she wiped her eyes, avoiding eye contact that might start her tears again. We stood, pushed our chairs in, and walked by her. We each put a hand on her shoulder as we walked by and went to our rooms. I lay on my bed, staring up at the ceiling. I kept thinking of my father looking around in the rear window of the car, a tear in his eye as he waved. I turned over and buried my face in the pillow so no one could hear me cry.

The next morning was Friday. When the school bus came, we weren't out at the gate. Mr. Mullins honked the bus horn a few times, and then drove off. None of us got out of bed until later in the morning. My mother didn't say a word about our missing school. She felt this was a time for us to be together and wanted us close to her in case we had any questions.

The house was quiet all day. Dick was sitting on the floor looking in the encyclopedia to learn about tuberculosis. Jim was at his desk, doing his paper delivery paperwork. When it was time for supper, we went into the kitchen and fed ourselves. Most of the afternoon my mother had been on the phone talking to our brothers and sisters about our father going to the sanitarium. Dick made a salad for my mother and warmed up two meatballs he found in the refrigerator and put them on a plate, in case she was hungry. None of us, Dick, Paul, Jimmy, or me, said a word to each other all day.

We walked around in a trance. We looked out windows and teared up when we'd see a picture of him on the piano or the one of him on the wall in the hallway.

After dark we went to bed again. I knelt by my bed and said prayers so my father would get better, not be in pain, and be home for my birthday or for Christmas or anytime, just so he came home.

The next morning, Saturday, my mother woke us up, smiling. She had made breakfast and asked us to come. It was on the table. It was like she was a new person. She told us God would answer our prayers. She got us out of bed and told us now was the time for us to be strong and that our father had been through worse than this in his life. With the Lord's help and our prayers, he would get through this, too.

THE BOY AND THE BIG WHITE ROCK

We were stunned.

"What was worse than this, Mom?" I asked.

My mother looked around at each of us.

"It was a difficult time for your father when his daddy fell off their barn roof in Minnesota. He died when your father was just a boy like you. Your father was the youngest of seven and so hurt by losing his father like that he could never bring himself to talk about it or think about it."

"Is Dad going to die, Mom?" I asked.

"All your father would want now is for you to do the best you can, in everything you do, and to go on with your lives just as he taught you. If you do that for him, it will give him the strength he needs to get well again."

We promised we would. I asked if I could write him letters.

"It'd be better to tell me things for him. I'm allowed to visit him, and I'd relay the things you want him to know and any other news from us. That way, he and I can talk longer during my visits, and I'd keep his spirits up. I could keep his mind busy with the things you want to tell him. It's important we make sure he keeps positive and wants to get better and come back home."

We understood this.

"I'm going camping," I said.

"In the snow?" Dick asked.

I ignored him, got up from the table, and went to my room to get dressed and get the lantern ol' Charlie Pitts gave me before he died. For some reason I felt like a grownup suddenly and not like a kid anymore. I couldn't explain the thoughts in my head. I was still 12, but overnight I was not the same as before, somehow.

I grabbed my knapsack and bedroll and headed out to the barn. Our horses, Jack and Major, were standing close to each other, keeping warm, soaking in the morning sun, not moving or eating their broken bales of hay lying on the ground before them. Horses could sleep standing up, so I wasn't sure if they were asleep. I slid the stable barn door open and went in, stuffed my knapsack with hay, and then got Jack's saddle down off the rack. I brought it to the opened doorway and put it on the floor. I started to get the saddle blanket when I paused and walked back to the door and looked out at Jack. Jack was a tall, gray gelding who loved a ride and to climb our hills. His winter coat was thick and feathery. He lifted his head and looked at me like he was waiting for me to make up my mind as to whether we were going with a saddle today or going bareback. It made no difference to him.

"Bareback," I said. I put the saddle on the rack and threw the saddle blanket over the stall door. I adjusted the straps on my knapsack, hooked the lantern to the straps, put it on my back, stepped out of the stable, and slid the door closed. I put Jack's bridle on and led him away. I needed enough space to jump on his back. At six-feet-tall, I didn't need the help of a cinder block to mount him anymore.

We rode the driveway and then down Cardner Road, across the small bridge and into the snow-covered alfalfa field. Jack raised his head high; his nostrils flared puffs of cold morning air. He shook his head as though he were waking himself up. He knew we were about to climb the steep hill to go to my campsite next to the spring behind the cliff. He liked camping with me. He was a smart horse, and he had an instinct his footing wouldn't be as sure on snow-covered ground.

We got to the back edge of the field. From there it was a steep climb. I grabbed a tight grip of his mane, held on and rode him up to see if I could stay on while he climbed the hill. Jack's thick coat helped my legs get traction, and the bare, leafless trees let me see ahead. I squeezed my legs and held a bunch of his mane in my fist. Jack's nostrils snorted steam every time his legs sprung forward like claw hammers, pulling us higher and higher, his hind legs pushing like springs, kicking snow until we reached the top. The trail to my campsite was more level from there. We got to the site and I slid off, dropping the reins to the ground.

I took off my knapsack and looked about the fire hole. It was covered in snow. I dragged my knapsack along a square patch of ground to brush the snow away. I packed the remaining snow to the ground with my feet. I gathered armfuls of dry leaves and made a mattress. I hung my knapsack on a tree branch and gathered fire logs and built a fire bigger than usual so there'd be heat glowing off for both Jack and me. When it was going strong, I gathered and stacked enough wood to take us through the night.

It was still daylight, so I mounted Jack and told him we were going for a ride.

We headed deep into the woods by the upper waterfall, which was frozen. A small amount of water was trickling over the falls, dripping down massive icicles that were melting slowly in the morning sun. I rode the woods to the back fence on our property line, and we turned left to go north. It was a longer ride than I had planned—a hike I had never done on horseback. When we came out of the woods into a clearing, we were across from where ol' Charlie Pitt's place was before they burned it down after he died.

I rode Jack to the edge of the field that faced across the road to Charlie's and we stopped. We stood there. Jack snorted puffs of steam. I remembered my friend, Charlie. I thought about the good times he and I had had together. How he let me play in his barn. How nice he was all the time. I thought of when he got sick, and my father would come back from work to drive him to a hospital in Rochester, so he wouldn't be alone for treatments before he died. I remembered the day he died. I wondered if ol' Charlie had tuberculosis like my father.

A tear frosted my eyebrow, thinking of what I would do if my father died. I pursed my lips, wishing ol' Charlie and my father could be there right then so we could go ice fishing at Pleasant Lake.

A breeze kicked up. Jack turned on his own and followed our tracks back to the camp. I took his bridle off and hung it over the knapsack. I stacked more firewood. I had my heavy coat, my corduroy pants, two blankets, a pile of dried leaves for a mattress, so, with the fire, I had all I needed to stay warm. I unbuckled the knapsack and pulled out a quarter bale of hay I had stuffed in it. I didn't pack any food for me. Jack leaned his head down, smelled the hay, lifted his head and turned toward me as if to thank me. He started munching. His back leg sprung as he relaxed. Horses can lock their knees. They will balance on three legs, resting one in case they have to move suddenly in the night. A horse's natural predator is the wolf. Their natural defense is speed. They keep one leg unlocked so they can move quickly.

I sat on a log by the fire and made some mourning

dove calls, trying to warm my hands.
"*Whoo—eee—who—who—who—*"
"*Whoo—eee—who—who—who—*"

I watched a squirrel carry an acorn up a tree and wondered where he had them buried for the winter.

Darkness came and I unrolled my blankets and sat down. I lay back and watched the stars over the creek side of the cliff, and listened to Jack munching his hay.

I saw the North Star behind a silhouette of a single dead leaf hanging from a branch and surrounded by the glow of a full moon above. I wondered what my father was doing at that exact moment.

Was he coughing a lot?

Was he losing weight? Would we ever go fishing again?

That night I made the decision I wasn't going to talk about this at school other than maybe to Holbrook and Judy Sessions. I could trust my friends. They wouldn't mention my father unless I told them I wanted to talk about it. School would never be the same again.

The next day a letter from my brother Fred at Cornell University was lying on my bed. In it he wrote that every week he was going to send me a new word to look up in the dictionary to learn and to use in a sentence in a letter he wanted me to send him back. The first word he sent was *pedantic*. I got the dictionary and looked it up. His second was *copious*. His third was *prevaricate*. This was fun. Every week his letters and new words and my dictionary time and writing him back kept my mind from worrying about my father—a little anyway—and I got to learn a new word.

On Saturday, I saddled Jack and rode down past Doc Webb's place to the end of the road and up the back hill on Route 80 to the big corner at Oran Delphi Road. Just across was Ted Dwyer's place, where Judy Sessions was living.

I rode across the Gooseville Corners and onto their snowy front yard, dismounted, and knocked on the door. Judy came out.

"Want to go for a ride?" I asked.

"Let me put a coat on. Want to come in?"

"Nah, I'll wait here."

When Judy came out, I mounted Jack, took my foot out of the left stirrup, and offered Judy a hand up. She got behind my saddle, her arms around me, holding on. I knew Judy was a few years older. I wasn't sure how old she thought I was, but it didn't matter to me, I liked her. At the moment, we were on my horse, crossing over Oran Delphi Road and riding back down the steep Route 80 hill to go to my house for some hot chocolate. We passed the Reynolds' place on the left, Don Chubb's house on the right, next door to that, Ed and Frank Butlers', and then, around a bend was Doc Webb's. The doc waved and shouted for me to check out his maple syrup cabin when I had a chance. I waved back as we rode on by.

My mother was at home. She welcomed Judy, and they talked about Baltimore while I warmed up some milk for hot chocolate. I had put Jack in the barn garage, still saddled, with half a bale of hay so he'd be okay for a while.

We drank hot chocolate and Judy and my mother

talked.

I walked Judy out back to see the waterfall. It was frozen over like an icy diamond crystal. We walked around the house to the barn. I brought Jack out of the barn to take Judy home. Before we mounted, Jack moved his head around and nuzzled Judy as if he wanted to say hello. He liked her. Judy put a hand under his chin and with the other she patted his nose and then scratched the side of his neck. They bonded their friendship.

On the way back to Ted Dwyer's, Judy rested her cheek on my back. I could hear her humming a song. I couldn't make it out, but I felt it and I liked hearing her voice. We didn't talk the whole ride back. She held me tight and kept her head on my back.

When we got to her house Judy slid to where she could reach her foot into the stirrup. I took my foot out. She grabbed the back of the saddle and swung around slowly. I turned to help and she paused, looked me in the eyes, and kissed me. She kissed me a wonderful long warm kiss. Her head tilted back—she looked in my eyes.

"I had fun today, Jerry. Thanks for thinking of me."

She lowered to the ground, rubbed Jack's velvety nose goodbye and ran to the house, waving just before she closed the door behind her.

I remember smiling and thinking if it weren't for my father being in the TB sanitarium, this growing up could be a good thing.

When I got home, I unsaddled Jack and stowed the bridle, saddle, and blanket. My world was shaken again when I walked in the house. My mother was packing a suitcase. She told me the sanitarium called while I was out riding and Dad might need surgery.

"They want to remove a part of his lung," my mother said. "I have to be with him a couple of days—keep his spirits up—while he goes through tests and we talk it over with the doctors."

My mother kept packing and instructed me to tell Dick to behave and be mature while she was away, and that she'd be back in a few days.

After my mother drove out, I went behind the swings and opened the door of my father's Oldsmobile. It hadn't been driven since he'd been gone. I sat in the driver's seat, thinking of him sitting there. I held the steering wheel like it was him driving. I could smell his cigarette tobacco. I wanted him to meet Judy Sessions. I got out, went inside and heated a tuna and noodle casserole for when Dick, Paul, and Jim got home.

I told them about Dad and the operation he might have to have—taking a part of his lung out.

When Dick said he didn't think someone could live without both lungs, I bolted around in a blind rage and ran toward him. I pushed him in a loud slam, his back against the wall so hard his head bounced off it.

"You take that back!" I screamed. "You take that back!"

Dick's nostrils flared as he stared at my fists, my clenched jaw and the tears in my eyes. I returned a dead cold stare. He apologized. We went to our rooms. I fell asleep without eating that night.

Judy and I went horseback riding as often as we could. I didn't know what love was, so we didn't talk about love. I just knew that when we were together, we were happy, and when we weren't together, we couldn't wait to be together again.

On Friday night I went to a school dance. We danced every slow dance. We square danced when they played one that sounded easier than most.

Judy told me she was praying for my father every day to get better. She was nice like that. I told Judy that I had to go spend three days at Cornell University. I was going to stay with my brother Fred at Delta Upsilon, his fraternity.

We had a long kiss goodbye that evening.

The weekend at Cornell was fun. Fred let me wear his sweater and called me "Joe College—big man on campus." I was able to leave the fraternity house without asking—walk over to the cafeteria and meet and talk to people. It was a lifetime memory for me. Fred drove me home.

When the car pulled up to the house I jumped out and ran to the barn. I saddled Jack and we trotted down to the Reynolds' place hill and up to Judy's. As soon as she opened the door, I took her by the hand, didn't say a word, and I led her out to Jack. I started to mount.

"Hold on a second, mister," she said.

She took my face in her hands and gave me a kiss.

"I missed you this weekend."

"I missed you," I said.

"Did you have fun at Cornell?"

"It was a lot of fun."

Judy and I rode for a couple of hours around the Conway, Penoyer, and Dwyer farms. We never stopped talking. I was telling her how nice the fraternity house was and what campus life was like. She told me about the book she read, letters she wrote to friends in Baltimore and that she was sad because she would have to leave soon. I didn't want to talk about that so we just rode. She held me close.

Chapter 16

"Never wrestle with pigs. You both get dirty and the pig likes it." ~ George Bernard Shaw

I had myself convinced I either wanted to be an Air Force pilot, an architect, or a pig farmer. Every time I mentioned an advocation at the dinner table, the next day after school I would find a number of books on my bed about the topic. One time my mother asked me to get in the car, and she drove me to Ithaca, to Cornell University and to a professor's office.

"Professor, Jerry here is showing interest in agriculture—"

"Pig farming," I interrupted.

Mother introduced us and explained that the professor was a professor of animal science.

"I'll leave you two alone to talk," my mother said. She stepped out into the hall.

The professor asked me why my interest in pigs, and what I knew about them. I shared what I had learned in encyclopedias about bedding them on a slant so the mothers could nurse their babies without lying on them. I told him what I knew about castrating a pig (although I didn't know why).

"Thank you for your time, Professor," my mother said.

"I'm impressed with the young man's knowledge of hogs, Mrs. Antil."

As Mother and I got ready to leave the professor handed my mother a piece of paper.

"This is an address of a pig farm. It's not out of your way," the professor said. "You might stop by, drive in and introduce Jerry to what the real pig business is about. Best the lad be sure he likes hogs."

The farm's barns and buildings were quite large and set back from the road. My mother pulled in the driveway, saw a man and woman talking. Our car pulled next to them and my mother opened her window. She told the couple that the professor from Cornell had sent us on an exploratory mission for her son. She pointed at me. The couple welcomed us as their guests. If memory serves me, we didn't get halfway up the dirt drive before the stench from pigs and hogs filled the car. We could hardly breathe, the smell was so bad.

"*P. U.* What's that smell, Mom?"

"Welcome to pig farming, son," my mother said.

"Let's go home," I said.

My mother didn't say a word—she didn't smirk or offer any judgment. She turned the car around.

When we got home, I thanked my mother for going out of her way to help me learn about pig farming. Dick came out of the house to tell my mother there was someone on the phone for her. After her call, my mother asked us to sit at the table, as she had some news.

"Your father and I thought it best not to worry you, so we kept it from you that he had his surgery last Friday."

"Is he okay?" I asked.

"I'm happy to tell you that your father is doing fine, and with prayers, he could be home soon if his healing goes well and has no complications."

I remember looking at my mother to see if her eyes were comfortable with what she was telling us, or if they were nervous eyes and maybe hiding some bad news. She was smiling. I believed her.

"The doctors make him cough several times a day to keep his lungs clear. It's painful for him to cough, but he knows he has to, so he does his best."

"Does he still have two lungs?" Dick asked.

"Yes. They only had to take the top portion of one of his lungs—so he still has two lungs."

I had grown since he went into the sanitarium.

"Will Dad even know me?" I asked.

My mother didn't answer. She just smiled.

We were so happy and couldn't wait to see our father again, after all this time.

There was a dance at the school that night. Judy Sessions was there. We danced all night, knowing that might be the last time we'd get to dance since she might have to move back to Baltimore any day.

Our family got busy during Thanksgiving with visiting family. Soon after I started receiving letters from Judy. Her parents had come during the school break and got her with no warning and gave her no time to say goodbye. She had moved back to Baltimore. She wrote me a letter I held all night. She signed her letter, "Love and Prayers, Judy."

I missed her. We wrote back and forth for months. I missed my father, too.

Chapter 17

"No matter what, I always make it home for Christmas." ~ Dolly Parton

It was the morning of Christmas Eve, but the house didn't have a festive feel as it had years before. There was snow on the ground. We always hoped for snow at Christmastime, and it was snowing heavily. The house seemed cold, still, and quiet.

I got out of bed and went to the kitchen wearing pajama bottoms and T-shirt. Dick was there with my mother.

"I'm making your favorite," my mother said.

It was poached eggs. My mother knew I loved poached eggs. I'd put one poached egg on a slice of buttered toast and eat it like an open-faced sandwich.

"Can you boys fold the clothes after breakfast so we could get ready for Christmas?" my mother asked.

We told her we would.

"Don and Mary (our sister) are coming today from Harrisburg. Dorothy (our sister) and Norman are coming in from Washington. Mike will be here from Lemoyne College and Fred from Cornell," my mother said.

My mother made no mention of my father. We were afraid to ask. We didn't want to make her cry. If our father wasn't there, that would have been the first Christmas without him. There wouldn't be a Christmas without my father.

We moped around the kitchen, eating, talking, and folding clothes as quickly as my mother piled them on the counter. It was almost two o'clock and I was still barefoot in my pajamas and T-shirt. Dick was in the living room looking at the pile of presents lying by the piano. Mike had come in and was sitting on the piano bench playing "Volga Boatman," which he had memorized.

I went to my room and fell asleep.

The next thing I remember, my mother was pulling on my toe. "Jerry, get up, get up."

I mumbled something.

"Your father's coming," my mother said.

"What!?"

"Your father's coming home!"

I had slept all day. I sat up rubbing my eyes. It was dark outside. My mother had a smile on her face. I wasn't sure if I was dreaming or really awake.

"Mike Shea just called and told me a man is driving your father home, and they stopped at the store and the driver went in to buy a newspaper," my mother said. "Mike Shea told me he went out to the car and said hello. He said he looks good, but he thought it would be nice to call us and let us know he was on his way."

I could hear Dorothy and Norm laughing and talking with Dick and Mike in the living room. I stood up. I brushed by my mother and went to the bathroom.

When I came out of the bathroom, I stood in the hall and looked through my bedroom window. I could see headlights coming up the drive. At first I thought it could be my father, but it was Mary and Don driving in with a Christmas tree tied on their car roof. I didn't think we were going to have a tree that year. I started to get dressed when the telephone in my father's and mother's room rang. I rushed in and picked it up.

"Hello?"

"Hello, is Jerry there?"

"This is Jerry."

"Jerry, this is Doctor Webb."

"Oh, hi, Doc."

"Merry Christmas, young fella."

"Merry Christmas, Doc. I saw your syrup cabin. It's really nice."

"Jerry, I thought you'd like to know that your daddy just drove past my place on his way home," Doctor Webb said.

"He did? He is?"

"I thought you'd like to know, what it being Christmas and all."

"I just heard he was coming," I said.

"Mike Shea called me with the news, too, son. Us old fogies have our own SOS system, don't ya know." He laughed. "We invented it. Have a *BULLY GOOD* Merry Christmas, son!"

I dropped the phone receiver on the floor and ran out through the dining room past Dorothy and Norm to the front door and pushed it open.

My mother shouted for me to put something on, but I was already out the door. I jumped off the porch barefoot and started walking quickly through the snow toward the gate, not taking my eyes off the hill at the top of the road by farmer Parker's. I was looking for the glare of headlights. I knew the car Dad was in would be coming over that hill at any minute.

Mary opened the window of their car as I scurried

past.

"Jerry, you'll catch your death, go put something on," Mary shouted.

I kept walking as fast as I could, and kept my eyes on the top of the hill.

Finally, almost to the gate, I saw the headlights of a car coming over the hill, inching slowly around the curve. The road had not been plowed, and it was slick, so they were taking their time coming down. I hopped out on Cardner Road. The car slowed to a stop and turned into the driveway, pausing next to where I was standing. The back window opened down halfway, and a hand came out for a shake.

It was my dad.

IT WAS MY DAD!

As the car began inching forward, I grabbed his hand and squeezed it, walking alongside.

"Jerry?" my father asked.

"Yes."

I started to cry. I'd grown so much since he saw me last, I wasn't sure he would recognize me. It frightened me to think my father might not recognize me.

"Remember us fishing at Little York Lake, Dad? Remember when I rowed our boat at Sandy Pond, Dad? Remember when you beat my airplane to Syracuse, Dad? Remember teaching me how to bake stuff? Make desserts, Dad? Can you remember me?"

When we approached the house, the family was outside on the porch, waving and cheering. He squeezed my hand.

"You caught croppies, Jerry me boy, we cooked

them at the Imperial House."

"Room Number Six, Dad."

"Room Number Six," my father answered.

He remembered me.

The car stopped and he got out slowly. He was still tender and healing from his lung operation. When he stood straight, he smiled at how tall I was. He ran his hand back and forth over my brush cut.

"You sure have grown, Jerry me boy. You sure have grown, son."

I stared in his eyes.

"I'm still the same, Dad. Just like you're still the same."

He shook my hand, put his arm around my shoulder, and we walked into the house with everyone cheering, laughing, crying, and happy again.

My mother barked.

"Go take a shower so you don't get frostbite."

"No! I'm not leaving my dad!" I barked back.

"Well, at least put some pants and shoes on."

I did do that. I got a sweater and came out and sat on the chair next to the couch my father was lying on, resting, smiling, watching everyone talking at once.

Don, Norm, and Mike were putting up the Christmas tree and Mary, Dorothy, and my mother were bringing out boxes filled with decorations and lights.

My father asked Dorothy for writing paper and a pen. He wanted to write friends in the TB sanitarium and wish them a Merry Christmas.

Watching my father, I remembered the night I laid on that same couch, the time I was poisoned from drinking the creek water after the dairy upstream poured toxic cleaning chemicals in it, killing the fish for miles. I thought of him sitting where I was sitting now—sitting tall, watching over me, his poisoned son—all night long, his silhouette crested by moonglow through a picture window.

Remembering that time, I sat up taller in the chair. I rested my head back and dozed off, exhausted from the stress and happiness. When I woke it was still dark outside. The house was quiet, and the lights were out except for the Christmas tree, a spectacular glow of lights and colors and shiny, sparkling decorations. The presents were stacked underneath. My father was still lying on the couch, but with a blanket over him. A pen rested in his limp hand and writing papers were on his lap, but he was sound asleep.

I got up and took the pen and paper off him and put them on my chair arm.

His eyes opened and he smiled.

"Can I have some water, son?"

I got a glass of water from the kitchen.

"Want a fire, Dad? I know how to build a good one."

"That would be nice, son."

I built a big fire with the largest logs. While I built the fire, I recalled the time I had left a tin garbage can lid filled with ears of harvest cow corn by the fireplace for Santa's reindeer.

I stacked wood, enough to take us through the night. I wasn't sure what time it was, but I knew everyone would be getting up soon. The family always celebrated

Santa's coming before dawn.

I warmed my hands by the fire and stepped back to the chair and sat down. He was asleep again. I took the water glass from his hand and set it on the floor beside him. I picked up his writing paper and pen from my chair.

I didn't read my father's entire letter, I read one page.

"I'm sleeping on the sofa, the first night home, just to be in the thick of things for Christmas in the morning. My boy, Jerry, is roughing it on a less comfortable chair right beside me while he and I catch up. He doesn't seem to mind. Watching him there makes me recall the many nights he would sleep in a bed roll over the falls here at Delphi Falls. The horses would come around grazing or just snooping far into the night.

Jerry didn't mind horses, woodchucks, squirrels, rabbits, foxes, deer, some bears, and a load of wild birds that roamed the upper falls some of the time."

I stopped reading.

I looked up at the glowing tree.

I looked over at the burning fireplace. I remember watching my father sleeping.

I felt a tear roll down my cheek.

"There is a Santa Claus," I said. "He came tonight."

Chapter 18

Eighth Grade Perdition – "If you're going through hell, keep going." ~ Winston Churchill

By the time my father had come home from the sanitarium I had my own room—and alone time to try to figure out what sex was. I'd sit on a fence and watch the horse try to mount a workhorse and wonder what sensation or satisfaction there was. Was it like kissing? I experimented with a ball point pen and my anus—one time only. Didn't get the connection. For all I knew girls had hair between their legs, and not much else. My eighth-grade classmates were a couple of years older than the tallest kid in school—me. How's that for freak? My father had his sons start school young, knowing we were going to be tall and look like the older kids. What a difference two years of age made in the brain of postwar innocence, and I felt in such an alone time I lost interest in everything.

Some school nights I'd sneak from the house, wade across the creek and climb the cliff up to the white rock. I'd sit on it, look down to see if I could see where the horses were grazing, and walk through the woods to my campsite next to the running spring. I'd build a fire. My iron skillet hung on a tree limb. I'd get it down and lay it on the fire and cook slices of Spam until they browned and I'd scramble eggs on top of the Spam while reading passages from the Bible sitting by the Coleman lantern. I left the skillet up there.

I wanted to be closer to God so I wouldn't mess up my confirmation with the bishop. If I understood it right, confirmation promised me passage into a new world of adulthood when he blessed my forehead with holy oil. At least I thought that's how it went. I'd stoke the fire to last through the night, fill the skillet with dirt for scrubbing in the morning. When I woke up, I'd scrub it, hang it, and douse the fire.

I wouldn't always go down to the house before school. Sometimes I'd climb down the back hill and go through the alfalfa field, cross the bridge to the front gate and catch the school bus without going to the house. In eighth-grade algebra I could smell my body odor while sitting at my desk. It was a different smell when I was taller. My armpits, my crotch— everything smelled and campfire smoke wasn't a cure. I hadn't lost interest in things, but until I could figure out this thing with my body, I wanted to be invisible. I found little interest in anything. I wanted to be in limbo. It was like I was in a freefall off one of our waterfalls.

I'd make daily climbs to the white rock on the hill across the creek, sit on it and study the seasons. The limestone creek below the white rock emanated from small natural springs above the two waterfalls and would trickle like a midday yawn in the heat of summer. But as months of winter ice melted the creek would rise to crashing crescendos, like thunder, as spring thaws rushed from both waterfalls and the side cliff's melting springs, carrying large shale rocks and railroad ties down its path as if they were floating feathers or fallen leaves.

A spring creek could rise many feet up on the sixty-foot-high cliff of blue/black packed shale on one side and the dirt-clay shoreline on the other side. Floating timbers and rocks eventually giving in to nature's power of water floated around and downstream. With the thaw, snow and ice would melt from trees lining the top of the cliffs, turning a woods of snow-covered crusts of white into a darkened Disney-like animated green of bark faces and arms of needled pines, giant oaks, overweight sugar maples and the insect-infected, dying elm. The creek's swell would rush down, carrying its portage under the bridge at the road and beyond.

Then it happened. One night I woke up in the dark groping myself into an unfamiliar climax. It was the first time I felt that sensation—half asleep, I was trying to replicate the feeling—when in the distance, headlights of a car turning into our driveway bounced off my varnished bedroom walls. It was a race between me repeating the climax experience and the car getting up the driveway to the house. I won. And my world would never be the same again.

Chapter 19

"Nothing changes until it becomes what it is."~ *Frederick Salomon Perls*

It wasn't as if the curtain had fallen on our weekly routine. We still went to the bakery on Saturday, and we still went fishing, but it was as if a giant scrim appeared on stage, masking my father's losses—his memory for one, a light cord to a year of his life, a part of his lung for the other. For me, my innocence needed no screen.

My father was on a death watch, searching for answers. Me? I was still trying to figure out the questions. Sitting next to him in the car, I missed Big Mike, the bakery man. My new dad wasn't a confrontational man. He wouldn't spar like the other dad. On drives to Sandy Pond or to Oneida Lake, we'd row out to fish, and I could see solitude in his eyes about his once love, the bakery.

While in the sanitarium it was inevitable that decisions at the bakery had to be made in his absence. With the death of his original partner, and then the tuberculosis, apathy took his heart out of the game. My father had tuned out—a bottle's cork becoming his diversion. Whatever decisions the bakery had made didn't matter to him anymore. He didn't care. My father and I could read each other's face, kind of like how a batter can read a pitcher's signal to the catcher and can sense the next pitch might be a curve ball, low on the outside.

My personal world had evolved to alarm bells ringing in my brain, a cacophony of mixed metaphors—from the reading of passages of the Bible nightly before turning to the wall and masturbating, trying to figure it out since the night the car headlights bounced off my room walls.

Our treks to the bakery had evolved. Oh, we'd still stop and cast lines in a lake or pond along the way or park near a fence to watch an enormous buffalo a farmer was trying to figure out what to do with, but our vibes as they once were had flopped our *friend-rich* quality time I believed we'd have forever.

The flop wasn't just my quest for learning about sex. That was the distraction. I was so out of reality I had actually convinced myself God turned his head when I turned toward the wall in bed. Leonard's Coffee Shop's kitchen with the naked Marilyn Monroe calendar added a few minutes to my picking up the bakery's mail from the post office.

I can remember my older siblings with their advanced educations passing my father off as beneath them intellectually. Sisters and brothers were old enough to be my parents. Some were so old I only remember them moving away from home in Cortland, taking with them things my father never had when he grew up, like private music lessons—piano, violin, clarinet—high school diplomas, and college degrees. Oh, they were lovely at holiday tables, but behind closed doors some would patronize his ninth-grade education. His success was the luck of a salesman—as if a career in sales embarrassed them. At this writing it still riles me, but dwelling on it more will only jaundice my story.

Chapter 20

"We will <u>bury</u> you!" Nikita Khrushchev

It's taken a lifetime of reflection to reassemble the infectious jigsaw pieces my father was juggling in the 1950s. Imagine a man who had witnessed two horrific wars—too young to have been drafted in World War I, the war to end all wars (1914-1918), and in the 1940s, too old to be drafted into World War II. Then came the 1950s, and the world was learning to live under new threats. This time, to my father it was personal. The world had become a combination of the worst of times. Not only was TB the number one killer, but suddenly there was the Cold War, a threat that could kill us all.

There were always a few days in the summer when the sun was so scorching it was painful. The day my father drafted my brothers Dick and me, complicit in something not one of us had done before, was one of those days. The next two days of shoveling and mixing what seemed like a hundred troughs of cement and wheelbarrowing them up a large plank to build a concrete bomb shelter attached to the side of our wood frame house was tantamount to an encyclopedia's etchings of Egyptian slaves pulling blocks of stone up the walls of pyramids.

My father's plan was that the flat roof of the bomb shelter would serve as a sun deck off the living room, as if it would mask the structure's hidden agenda, its fictional purpose of withstanding a hydrogen bomb blast. My mission was to conspire to the coverup by painting the deck's wooden rails a canary yellow with the paint I had borrowed to paint my bicycle in honor of *She Wore a Yellow Ribbon's* Olivia Dandridge, my unrequited love. The weekend ended with me in bed with heatstroke and a completed bomb shelter.

Concrete deck on side of house was our bomb shelter.

The peeling deck rail and cracks in the poorly mixed cement were noticeable and popping up like sand crabs on a beach when my sister Dorothy called the house in 1956, in tears. She and her husband, a merchant marine captain who was decorated with a Meritorious Service Medal for bravery in WWII, just had a new baby girl the week her husband's cargo ship went aground on a coral reef near Bermuda. It was uninsured, leaving him jobless.

"I'll call you right back," my father said.

He hung up, picked up the receiver.

"Operator," the local exchange operator said.

"Myrtie, please get me our Mary in Little Rock."

"Hi, Mr. Mike—of course," Myrtie said.

He gave Myrtie the number.

My sister Mary answered the call.

"Mickey, how much does your Don take home per week, do you know?"

"You mean, his pay?"

"Yes."

"I think fifty dollars, why?"

"No reason. Thank you, honey—we'll talk soon."

My father hung up and then called Dorothy's husband, told him he was thinking about putting a swimming dam near the house and offered him fifty dollars per week to build it.

"Bring the family."

"Mike, there's a beautiful swimming hole in your back yard, under the falls," my sister's husband said.

"Oh, that's fun swimming for the kiddos," my father said. "I'm thinking of a spot for Mommy and me."

A six-by-six-foot concrete dam spanning twenty-four feet across the creek got built, and my brother-in-law was able to interview for jobs during downtimes. He ended up accepting a job with the U.S. Public Health Department for $50 a week. That was the upside of building the dam.

Every early indication showed that the dam was a success. Its upstream slope would fill with water when the spillway's slush boards were inserted in its middle. We swam behind it for several weeks until one night we forgot to remove the spillway's slush boards and a heavy, all-night rainstorm caused the creek to swell, rapidly eroding the clay that braced one side of the dam. The water gnawed the bank back more than three yards away from the dam, leaving two large blocks of concrete, like cemetery stones making the creek look like Monument Valley in a John Ford western.

It was a scene forever captured in solid concrete that would seed verbal jibes from some of my pious intellectual siblings as to how ill-conceived Dad's dam folly was. To me, not one of my older siblings was sensitive enough to grasp that building the dam was the method my father used to give his son-in-law work—not charity, but a dignified means of putting food on his table.

Years later, while researching for a Louisiana murder mystery novel I was writing, I found solemn reprieve for my father's dam, learning that the U.S. Corps of Engineers spent hundreds of millions of dollars building levees (dams) down the Mississippi, many of which tragically failed, flooding towns under suffocating layers of silt and burying inhabitants alive.

It was during the "year of the dam," when my college-bound brother, Dick, had been invited to preview Syracuse University during a celebrated football weekend. He was considering Syracuse, the alma mater of our two sisters and both of their husbands.

"Dick, be a gentleman. Don't crack wise. Try to make a good impression," my mother told him.

Dick was not a role model. He fought being a good student. When he was young, he was tested with a near genius IQ. The problems began when somebody told him his IQ and he played on it as if it were divine provenance, becoming a classroom lethargic no-account, above it all. Schooling was just a misadventure. He was a charming guy, but he had a knack for going out of his way to look for trouble. He left the house in suit and tie, then pulled his car over and parked on Pompey Hollow Road and changed into leathers he had hidden in the trunk and drove to Archbold Stadium and the Syracuse/Colgate football game, where he managed to get into a fight with Colgate students in the stands. They took the fight outside. He and six others with him lost the fight. They were tied to chairs and their heads were shaved. Dick's shaved bald head was crowned with the letter C. In his hand was a newspaper clipping with a photograph looking down at seven young men sitting in chairs, their heads spelling out COLGATE.

It was the first time I saw my normally unflappable and one-step-ahead-of-the-law brother in tears, sitting in his black leather jacket, leather pants, and boots with ankle chains. My mother shipped him off to Joliet Junior College in Illinois, thinking being away from home might help him mature. The fact that the junior college was near the Joliet Prison was metaphorical. It had no bearing on her decision.

It was during that period—the dam year—when I began sensing our family's gathering freefall. My father's TB saga floated on thermals, like haunted balloons that don't come down or burst, but hover like a death watch. My mother respected the man from the day they met. She adored him and the ground he walked on. With empathy for what he was going through emotionally, my mother would turn a blind eye to his drinking bouts. He was a discreet drinker. He disguised it in his coffee throughout the day and never drank before driving. And if he felt out of sorts, he'd take a nap.

Chapter 21

"Sometimes it's good to get off the merry-go-round and get on a rollercoaster." ~ Gareth Pugh

And so, the fog began rolling in—in heavier layers. One Saturday morning my father and I went to the bakery. I spent precious moments staring at the naked Marilyn Monroe calendar on Leonard's Coffee Shop kitchen wall while my father was up in his office, reading business mail. I thought we were on our way home when he made an unannounced turn and drove us to a town I had never been to before. He pulled onto a paved area and we parked in front of a Distelfink Soft Ice Cream stand. He introduced me to the man who owned it. The man was franchising the soft ice cream concept. They talked for a short time and the man handed me a vanilla cone. As we drove home, my father told me he was selling his bakery interest and starting a stand.

"An ice cream stand?" I asked. "Where?"

"Not sure, son. I'm thinking Route 11. Carvel could use some competition." (US Route 11 was known for heavy passenger/commercial traffic.)

"Will you still have the bakery, Dad?"

He pulled a check from his pocket and showed it to me. It was made out to him for a large amount of money.

"Already sold it, son. Just giving them a month to tie up loose ends."

"Does Mom know, Dad?"

"She will when we get home, son."

"Why can't we keep the bakery?"

"None of the older kids wanted it," my father said.

"I want it," I said.

My father watched the road, as if in thought.

"What would you have done with it, son?"

"I'd figure it out. I don't know, but it'd be better than earning a buck-fifty a week mowing lawns," I said.

Hearing that, my father drove through Tully, not turning on Route 80 like we normally would to go home to Delphi Falls. He drove straight to downtown Syracuse and parked at the curb next to the towering, historic Hotel Syracuse.

"Come with me, son."

We went in the hotel, and my father led me through a hall to a service elevator by a kitchen. We rode it to the basement. The elevator door opened to windowless, dark, concrete hallways with long fluorescent bulbs attached to the ceiling. In the center was a glass-paneled island, an enclosed office. The door was lettered, MR. BLOOM, PRODUCE MGR. My father opened the door and we stepped in.

"Hi Mike," Mr. Bloom said.

"Mr. Bloom, I'd like you to meet my boy, Jerry. Jerry, shake hands with Mr. Bloom."

Mr. Bloom and I shook hands.

"Mr. Bloom, Jerry's looking for a summer job. He's a good worker. He won't let you down."

Mr. Bloom never asked my age, not knowing I was underage. I assumed with my six-foot plus height, he didn't give it a second thought. He reached into a side drawer, opened it and pulled out an employee time card. He asked if Jerry was with a G or J. He wrote my name on the card and pointed to the hall at a time clock.

"Jerry, your card will be in that clock over there. Your work days are Sunday through Thursday. You have Fridays and Saturdays off. You'll work eight to four, with ten-minute coffee breaks, one at 10 a.m. and then at 3 p.m. You have half an hour lunch at noon—bring one. Start tomorrow. Ask for Red when you get here. Red's your boss," Mr. Bloom said.

"Thank you, sir," I said.

"Any questions, son?" Mr. Bloom asked.

"What's the job, Mr. Bloom?" I asked.

"Starting tomorrow, you'll be a sanitary engineer. Ninety-five cents an hour. Welcome aboard, son."

In the day, you could buy a reliable, working used car for $30. With one handshake, at 15, I was earning $38 a week all summer mopping floors, carrying garbage, and incinerating newspapers and magazines the housekeepers collected from the rooms.

There were so many girlie magazines and naked playing cards sent down on Sundays their titillating edge wore off and I stopped setting them aside or fanning through them before tossing them in the furnace. My sexual awakening at the Hotel Syracuse was observing behavior between female waitresses and housekeeping staff and the male chefs and cooks, coming from their locker rooms in the basement and waiting for the elevator. I could overhear my boss, Red, talking of going to Utica to play the horses and to visit the red-light (brothel) district.

That magical summer I was oblivious to the outside world. There was an implied independence that came with earning a paycheck—much like the drafting of 17-year-olds during WWII. Someone would drive me to work, someone would be there to pick me up and drive me home or drop me off at Bob Holbrook's when I had carton boxes filled with burned-out light bulbs for plinking with our .22 and BB gun.

"Jerry, why don't you stay here tonight? My dad can drive you to work in the morning when he goes in to Syracuse," Bob said.

He shared the room with three brothers. There were two beds. I took a blanket from the end of one of the beds and started making a palate on the floor.

"What're you doing?" Bob asked.

"I'm making a palate," I said.

"Why?"

"I'm going to sleep on the floor," I said.

"Sleep with us," Bob said.

"I like sleeping on the floor," I said.

"You're sleeping with us. Get in bed," Bob said.

I took him by the arm and nudged him to the window.

"Bob, I wet the bed," I whispered. "Let me sleep on the floor."

Bob stepped back pondering, his brow furrowed.

"Oh, you won't wet the bed here, Jerry," Bob said.

"How do you know I won't?"

"Cause Ronnie and I'd kick the living shit out of you."

I slept in the bed and stopped wetting that night.

On days off, Bob and I had two routines. One was driving to North Syracuse to watch the ongoing construction of the Distelfink Ice Cream stand my father was morphing—everyday a new costly surprise—from an ice cream stand to an ice cream stand plus a diner with a jukebox plus an upstairs in case someone had to sleep over. The front of the restaurant was going to be glass that would curve out in a half circle to display the new soft ice cream machine.

One day Bob and I drove in just as a bulldozer accidentally knocked one of the long cinder block walls completely over and it landed on a stack of glass panes for the front of the restaurant. Holbrook backed up and we drove away unannounced.

Our alternate summer routine, aside from talking about our both becoming forest rangers and the bounty for a mountain lion pelt, was the burrowing woodchuck, each den a nightmare for farmers. Their numerous holes and tunnels were breaking the legs of livestock. Once considering the woodchuck a possible food source, Bob caught one, dressed it and cooked it to find it an abysmal bitter taste. He and I would spend my days off from the hotel walking country roads. Once we walked eight miles to Fayetteville to buy Bob an electric razor on sale for $14 for his four whiskers. That summer, between us, we shot eighty-six woodchucks.

Chapter 22

"Wisdom is always an overmatch for strength."
~ Phil Jackson

The conundrum was although aggressively inching well over six-feet-tall, I had little interest in playing the tall fellow's sport, basketball. I was a towering 14-year-old sophomore—tallest kid in school. And to me, my playing basketball would be a charade, a ridiculous cliché. What turned my head was its side benefits, like the bus rides to and from away games with cheerleaders. On court, basketball was a bore, but my game was in its periphery, celebrating the seasonal celebrity of being tall. I got a flat top brush cut like the pro Johnny Kerr of the Syracuse Nationals, and I adopted an athlete's superstition, eating a poached egg sandwich before games. And there was the kissing on away-game buses.

My father never saw me play, but he assumed I was good, and felt my height might open doors for me. While his Distelfink Ice Cream parlor and diner were still under construction in North Syracuse he arranged to build a large barn at the falls, complete with a hardwood floor, two backboards, rims and nets. The barn had steel cable rafters as opposed to conventionally hewn wood beams, so the high arc of shooting basketballs wouldn't be hindered.

It was during this time I could feel my confidence in my prospects come into focus as a possibility. My memory isn't clear as to how it came about but there I was, looking old enough to buy beer and embarrassed being the only sophomore required to play on the Junior Varsity basketball team.

Dad attached the barn with hardwood floor to the stable.

Paul Smith College, in far northern New York, expressing an interest in my playing for them and going to their forestry school. The college invited me to spend a school break weekend on campus as its guest. My father arranged for me to hopscotch bakery trucks along routes that would eventually get me dropped off at the college near the Vermont border. I can remember there were no passenger seats in the bread trucks, and I had to stand most of the way. It took riding three bread trucks to their distribution centers and one tractor trailer delivering a bulk load of bread to an army base to carry me 188 miles to Paul Smith College's food hall's kitchen door. The plan was that my father would come on Sunday to pick me up and drive me home.

THE BOY AND THE BIG WHITE ROCK

The college campus was breathtaking. The people were friendly, down to earth, real. I was in awe of their Forestry School and the Resort School Management College. I remember feeling grown up while walking around the campus and meeting professors and students. The college felt to me like it was in another world. There were no traffic lights, no city sounds. It was almost as if it was a privilege just being there, as close to heaven as one could get while being alive. It was the largest college campus in the world, resting on a quiet peak overlooking 14,000 acres of smokey, wooded, rolling hills.

When Sunday came, my day was spent waiting for my ride home. It was dark when I saw my brother Dick's white Plymouth convertible coming up a hill and into the entrance to the college. I was a bit confused. Dick was away at junior college in Illinois, and it'd be rare for anyone to use his car in his absence.

As it approached, I could see Bob Holbrook was driving. I walked out to meet it. I opened the passenger door. My father was leaning back in the rear seat. He lifted his head. He smiled and gave me a muffled welcome before lowering his head back. In the driver's seat, Bob stared through the front windshield with pursed lips. My best friend was making a point to let me know he was blind and deaf to the moment. He didn't say a word, not even a *hi*, implying the moment wasn't any of his business. He gestured for me to get in, that he would drive.

My respect for my father and what he had been through with tuberculosis and the death of his friend and partner was unconditional. I remember my mind making it a point that night to block negative thoughts, like why wasn't he driving and why we weren't in his Oldsmobile. The answer to each was apparent to me, but I remember the moment and consciously choosing not to delve. I was grateful for all my father had gone through to get me to the college in the first place, and for the barn and for being my confidant since my early childhood.

Bob shared my deep respect for my father. He kept his eyes on the road as if he and I were in another room and he riddled me with questions about Paul Smith's forestry college and its curriculum, and did I meet any girls. He was helping fill the void of an awkward moment. It was a long drive, a long moment, and I remember him nudging me awake as we slowed down to turn onto Berry Road, nearly home for him. He drove to his house and pulled over. He nodded for me to get out and go around to drive. He left the car running and stepped out. As I walked around the car, he took my arm and leaned near my ear.

"Your pop's worried about something, Jerry."

"What?"

"I'm not sure. I gave him his space—I let him sleep."

"Why this car?" I asked.

"It was parked at the Distelfink," Bob said. "I drove to North Syracuse to see how the construction was going and to ask if anybody knew when you were coming back. Your father was sitting at the counter with a cup of coffee but in no condition to drive. He asked me if I could drive him up to get you."

"Thanks, buddy. I'll tell you about Paul Smith tomorrow," I said.

Don't be too hard on your old man," Bob said.

I got in the car and drove my father home.

Chapter 23

"Magic is the art of making dreams come true."
~ Doug Henning

I wrote the nonfiction, *Home on the Range,* that went into revealing detail about how, when the world was young, my father wanted to be on stage, maybe in Vaudeville, storytelling and performing magic. It was the early 20th century and he was a teen at the time and a popular babysitter and swimming instructor at a posh hotel casino on a lakeshore in Minnesota during the summer months. When he was married with eight of his own children, he'd entertain us, whether distracting us from a devastating, unpredictable world at war, or from seeing the Army and Navy uniforms everywhere. At an age when I was entering my early teen years, most kids got a birds and bees talk.

Me? My talk was a lecture about the secrets of performing a magician's misdirection.

"Son, everyone knows magic is a trick, but the trick to magic is to guide your audience's attention away from a secret action," my father would say.

I remember the night at the dinner table when my father and mother announced that during the upcoming summer months, they were going to use the barn to start a summer day camp for inner city kids. My mother would run it. Through word of mouth my father had already interested parents and enough kids to fill a bus that would bring them to our Delphi Falls weekday mornings for arts, crafts, nature walks, horseback rides, warm meals, naps, and being read to before being driven home at three.

This was a delightful, fulfilling summer for my mother and, as I would learn, a compassionate, successful, misdirection by my father. A summer day camp for needy urban kids was his magic wand. He wasn't lying to us or himself about the stressful financial situation he was in. He was just buying time. Having been tagged a day camp counselor for no pay but all I could eat, my summer was about to be busy lifting three kids up on Jack's bare back, holding the reins and walking horseback rides to the falls, snapping a Kodak picture of the riders in front of the waterfall and walking them and Jack back to the barn for the next load.

On my Saturdays off, I would drive over to Holbrook's on Berry Road and Bob and I would slide down his falls or go for full-moon walks and talks. One night we walked eighteen miles up and eighteen miles back just to see the new, double-decked Greyhound scenic cruiser bus. We followed the North Star and talked of forestry, of Paul Smith College, if anyone would come up with a cure for the Dutch Elm disease, or what a girl's breast might feel like. Bob would make a point of telling me what a close friend I was, and he'd imply he was giving me free rein—like he didn't want me to lower my sights and dreams waiting for him. He told me he saw bigger things in my future than standing in a forest ranger lookout tower. He was an amazing person and friend. He would speak confidently about his future, as if he knew his time would come and he was okay waiting for it.

The summer ended with a happy sense of fulfillment for my mother. Her choice of destinies was to educate and counsel the young. For some reason, the summer day camp had dulled the anxiety the building of the restaurant had wound so tight. The distraction of the summer day camp worked. In fact, there were several days when my father was at home, not leaving the house, not consumed with the construction of the Distelfink Ice Cream stand and Diner, not traveling to North Syracuse.

He made and received a noticeable number of telephone calls. The telephone was in his and my mother's bedroom. I don't remember the pretense, but one day one of my brothers—I can't remember which—and I were called into their bedroom. My parents were resting back on their bed—as they did when watching television in their room —*The Jack Benny Show* or Groucho Marx's *You Bet Your Life* quiz show. My mother, with a searching smile asked, "What would you boys think about having a new baby brother or sister?"

In my naivety, her grin told me she was so fulfilled after a summer of working with children that she wanted another child. It was years later, recounting my mother and father's grins on their faces, it likely meant they had had a private married moment.

"Have you had that talk with the boys yet?" my mother asked my father while we were standing there. My father was as embarrassed as we were. My mother got up and left us to our privacy.

"Boys," my father said, "When you get in the shower, wash down as far as possible, wash up as far as possible—then wash possible."

He cackled.

I remember shaking my head and my mother's voice coming from the hall like she was giving us a salad recipe:

"Wash your foreskin."

When we left their bedroom, my mind was a blank, looking for a dictionary to look up *foreskin*. I can't speak for my brother. As we stepped out, the telephone rang and my father picked it up.

Years later, I was telling one of my sisters about his sex talk. She told me his talk to his daughters was, "If you get in trouble, bring the baby home. We'll raise it."

Chapter 24

"No one ever drowned in sweat." ~ Lou Holtz

My father's sleight of hand—his creation of the summer day camp as a plausible diversion—worked. Along with it, everything at home appeared to be back to normal. The evolution of my father's semiretirement felt natural. I was too immature to read the real tell signs—like what his being in a suit and tie again meant after a period of his dressing casually. I had forgotten the unspoken signals of the 1940s during the war, when soldiers on furlough or at rest wore fatigues. When they boarded buses, trains and planes and were going back to battle, they donned their uniforms and ties.

For me school was about to start. It was my junior year and the memories of spending time with my father during that period where he was wearing his suit and tie again was the ride with him to see the work going on at the Distelfink. He pulled in front of the restaurant with painters on ladders outside. He gave me the grand tour. He showed me the expensive new walk-in cooler and a large automatic coffee maker and refrigerated milk dispenser. He opened a small crate of cooking utensils for the new short-order grill.

"Son, this is the short-order grill on this side. Over there on that side is the salad or condiment bar. Always cook and plate here—have whoever's working the salad bar add the condiments over there and then they would serve it."

"Got it," I said.

He handed me a quarter to put in the jukebox and another to play the pinball machine after my tour. I remember Elvis Presley singing *All Shook Up* while I was looking at the unfinished stairs leading up to the second floor and my father not making mention of them or of the second floor at all, for that matter. I can remember his standing in the shadow, like a ghost about to depart, watching me take everything in. He stepped outside and held the door for me. Before going to the car, we walked to the entrance of the Distelfink parking lot on the Route 11 frontage. He stood, his arms folded, watching traffic go by. He stared north up to the highway's horizon, in a glaze and as if he were talking to himself:

"It's coming," he said.
"What's coming, Dad?"
"A mile up," my father said.
"What's a mile up, Dad?"
"Thruway's coming, son."
"What's that?"
"The New York State Thruway."
"Through here, Dad? Through where? I heard about it, the Thruway."
"It's going to cross Route 11. It'll reroute everything. Opens in a month."

He unfolded his arms and rested his hands on his hips.

"Won't that be good, Dad, the Thruway?" I asked.

"Businesses on Route 11 will be buried alive," my father said.

I couldn't grasp the depth of what he meant at the time, but what I was about to learn was that soliloquy about "being buried alive" was my father's funeral psalm for Route 11 and an epitaph for the flushing of his money in an out-of-control money pit called Distelfink.

After we got home, my father disappeared, and I wouldn't see him near the Distelfink soft ice cream parlor, diner, and coffee shop ever again.

My junior year in high school—I was 15—was distracted by basketball practice and games, cross country practice, tournaments and a junior prom. For news about my father's whereabouts, I'd read my mother's eyes and let that radar tell me if he was okay. It was as if I was in a zone—like I was always on court. Offense and defense had become my only paths, and I wasn't differentiating between being an anal oriented athlete and a concerned son.

The academic year of 1956-57 was soft-focused as well. I took Donna Cerio to our junior prom. I remember basketball practices, the showers after games, flunking Latin and physics, and not doing well with most classes with the exception of English and my second year in algebra. Small town's rumors echo, and I could hear them the day our student guidance counselor called me to her office. She asked me what my plans were after high school. I told her I didn't know. She took a piece of paper and drew a wide triangle with one point reaching the top of the page.

"Life is a forest, Jerry. Picture this triangle as life."

I stared blankly at the triangle.

"Think of these as trees in a forest, Jerry."

She drew a line across the middle of the triangle, cutting it in half.

"There are tall trees in the middle—see them? The shorter trees are out to the side—can you see those?"

I nodded.

"Jerry, you're a shorter tree, on the outside—out here."

"What's that mean?" I asked.

"It means you won't be disappointed if you don't expect too much—like don't consider trying to get into college. Consider alternatives, like being a truck driver—maybe a school bus driver—perhaps an Army career is for you. There is nothing wrong with being a short tree, Jerry. Not everyone can be a tall tree. It's important you understand."

I remember leaving the student counselor's office thinking I could never trust an adult. I would make my own decisions, go my own paths. Good or bad. They would be my paths. Would I ever ask advice and listen? Yes, but from the moment I pulled that woman's door closed behind me I've never let an adult tell me what I could or couldn't do with my life.

Between the rigors of basketball, cross country, and bogus guidance counseling, my search for answers about the world of sex in 1956 was put on a back burner. My basketball world blossomed handsomely for a number of years with the diversions of celebrity my height gave me, so I subconsciously put my *birds and bees* quest in an extended time out. Oh, there were still the bedtime turns to the wall, but they had become more perfunctory than they were Marilyn Monroe calendar moments. My sexual awakening would have to wait.

As to the world I was living in, it was out of sight, out of mind, and I sometimes thought about my father, wondered where he was, what he was doing. I remember older siblings telling me my father was unemployable. At his age (56), nobody would hire an old man. I'd listen in denial, put their assessment of my father's future right up with my guidance counselor's telling me to become a truck driver. I assumed my father was okay, traveling, consulting with bakeries.

It was well after dark the night the bus brought me home from a late practice. We had been scrimmaging for an upcoming playoff game. The house was quiet inside, and my dinner waited for me on the table. Next to the plate was a *Baker's Weekly,* a business magazine my father read. I pulled its cover open. Its first page was a full-page advertisement that, with the exception of one sentence in the middle, was blank:

MIKE ANTIL TO COME OUT OF RETIREMENT

My first thought made me smile. It was a feeling my father had to be famous for that to appear in a magazine—and in a stretch of mixed messages I could feel certain things about to get sorted, and maybe our family might soon be in the normal chaos it once thrived on.

As to my basketball prospects, my parents were always supportive—how many kids had their own basketball court to practice in? —but they were never at my games. I took it they weren't sports fans. During my father's absence my mother kept a smile on her face—meaning it, confident that things would work out, and she'd feed my superstition and make my poached egg sandwich before every game. Years later—she was 93 when she passed—I learned what a big child star my mother was on the figure-skating rink—in ice shows that traveled nationwide. Photos and costumes and newspaper articles about her prowess were on display after her funeral. My sisters shared with us that my mother and father felt their children would get more out of life from experiencing our own life events and not living in their parent's shadows. They chose not to attend our games for our own growth.

I remember looking at the picture of my mother in costume, at 12, twirling on a block of ice, and thinking the basketball team I played on my junior year in high school was the only Fabius Central varsity basketball team in the 1950s to win a championship. I remember smiling, the barn, the poached egg sandwich and two lifelong friends. Holbrook, a junior along with me and Marty Bays, a senior on the team who volunteered to tutor me in physics. My memories of that basketball season are fuzzy, like snowflake flurries at dusk. On court, in the shower, or on the bus rides home, I was a robot.

School let out for the summer. Not only was I about to be a senior the next fall, I was unaware that I was getting on my last Fabius Central School bus ride home with a sense there was something in the wind. I felt a family transition moment coming. I couldn't quite put my finger on what form it would be in, and I was afraid to ask. I do remember my confidence in my parents protecting their young as if we were bear cubs. The survival instincts of my mother and father were equally honed. They were both intelligent, thoughtful, excellent managers, and not afraid of snakes along life's path. I felt I knew my father better than anyone. I knew my father's absence was out of necessity and I knew he wasn't off on a drinking binge. He never drank while he worked trying to put food on the table—only when he was alone at night. I treated his being gone as if he had gone foraging for food that would keep his family through the winter. All I could do was wait for the next curtain to go up.

Chapter 25

"I would ride with you upon the wind..." ~ Yeats

One man, a much-spoken-about character in our past who shall go nameless in this accounting, lived in the Fabius surrounds. He was the area drunk. Dating back into the nineteenth century, his family controlled a major foundry. The man was an officer of the company and such a drunkard the company paid him an enormous salary just to stay away. They paid him so much he owned a mansion, sports cars, and always a new Cadillac. Rumor had it he once bought an expensive horse, couldn't train it to do his bidding, so he pulled a revolver and shot it.

Another time, late one night my brother Dick and his friends were gathered in front of the Hastings' general store on Oran Delphi Road in the small crossroad hamlet of Delphi for secret drag races with their parents' cars (without their parents' permission) when this man's long black Cadillac pulled up and turned in under the gas station's sign. The man got out, pulled a wad of fifty-dollar bills from his shirt pocket, waved them and announced he'd race anyone.

"Cherry Valley and back—who's got what it takes?" he slurred.

Cherry Valley was at the corner of Oran Delphi Road and Route 20, two and a half miles away. Out of empathy, none of the young crowd responded. The only sounds in the air were from croakers and crickets. He sneered, stuffed the bills in his shirt pocket, harumphed, got back in his Cadillac, started it, and stomped on the gas pedal. The rear tires were on a bed of sharp black cinder under the sign and one tire spun until it began to smoke, melting the tread, which came flying off like a shooting rubber band. The man got out of the car, walked back and kicked the rim. Dick and his friends changed the tire for him while he sat in his car without saying a word and then drove away.

I tell you that story so you will understand this one.

When school let out for summer vacation there always seemed to be a day of reckoning—as if a few months of downtime was upon us, and what were we going to do about it? The sun was settling down and Paul and I were sitting on the swings by the empty flagpole in the front yard. He was swinging, I was twirling around in my swing, but we both were conjuring what to do all summer.

We watched a car come through the gate and leave a billowing trail of our driveway road dust. It was that same man's long black Cadillac. He sped toward the house, slowed to a stop, and parked cautiously thirty feet away from the front door. He got out of his car, stretched his arms out in a yawn and then scratched his head, as if he was thinking what approach he might use. Like a gunslinger in a cowboy movie, he stood as if he was looking over barroom doors to scope for varmints inside before pushing them open and going in. He didn't notice us on the swings. He reached in through his car window, took out an unopened bottle of champagne, sauntered up to the house and knocked.

He knocked several times. When my mother opened the door, he raised the bottle in an offering gesture. My mother said something we couldn't hear clearly, and she started to close the door. Its movement paused, perhaps caused by his foot, then it opened again, wide, and this time she came out. Not uttering a word, she pointed at his car, as if telling him to leave. At six foot, my mother towered over the man. We could hear the man telling her, *"Heard Big Mike was coming home. Just came by to say hello."*

Without so much as a blink, my mother grabbed the drunkard's ear, marched him to his car, opened its door, put him in and slammed the door closed. She pointed to the gate.

"Leave!" my mother barked. "Now!"

His car backed away, turned and headed down the drive and out through the gate.

"And don't bother coming back!"

My mother turned to go to the house and looked our way.

"Your father's coming. Find Dick and Jimmy," my mother said. "I want everyone at the table—no excuses."

I could tell my mother was disoriented and anxious—as if she hadn't had time to gather her thoughts after having to learn from the town drunk that my father was on his way home, and she didn't know what surprises to expect next.

"Dick's in Syracuse, Mom," Paul said.

My brother Dick had dropped out of Joliet Junior College in Illinois, grown long sideburns, and chain-smoked king-size Pall Mall cigarettes. Dick was always good with money. He could make a dollar stretch. He sold his Plymouth convertible and opened a savings account. He got a morning job on an assembly line at the EASY Washing Machine Company in Syracuse and, for transportation, he spent his nights driving a taxicab, learning city haunts and getting to know the city's softer underbelly—from back alleys with their bricked in secrets to the sinners who would crawl out from their darkness when the moon was full. Driving night shift in a cab was Dick's hall pass behind city curfews.

"Well, find Jimmy," my mother said.

"Mom, I've gotta go to Delphi," Paul said. "JoAnne needs me. I promised." My brother Paul's summer was toast already. He was in love with a girl in Delphi.

"Where's Jimmy?" my mother asked.

"He's delivering his newspapers, Mom," I said. "I'll be there." *Grit* was a farm newspaper Jim had distribution rights to. That kept him busy when he wasn't selling popsicles and Eskimo pies in Delphi.

A blank look came over my mother's face. She turned and went inside.

Chapter 26

"Not my good china, Mike." ~ Mary Holman Antil

There was a serving platter in the middle of the dining room table piled with a stack of egg and black olive sandwiches. My mother was sitting at her end of the table, her hands clasped, waiting and whispering to herself what sounded like forgivable speculations as to reasons why she had no knowledge or warning of my father's pending visit or what it was about. *"We should welcome him home, be quiet and listen—not interrupt,"* were among her more audible thoughts. I went into the laundry room and grabbed a bag of potato chips from a carton box, left over from our Snook's Pond summer enterprise. I stepped back to the table, ripped it open and sat down. I reached for a sandwich just as the reflections of car headlights bounced through the living room's darkness as they approached the house from the gate.

I had my half sandwich almost gone when the front door opened. My father's entrance coming in the house and into the light of the dining room in suit and tie was as matter-of-fact as a ship's captain would bust in to address his crew in the officer's mess to announce a gale storm coming and what to do about it so everyone could man a station. He offered no formal greeting or smile; he paced about as if the meeting was a necessary interruption to a whirlwind he was riding on.

"They'll be here at eight. The crowd will start coming at eleven, is my guess," my father said.

"Who'll be here, Mike, what crowd?" my mother asked.

I stuffed the last bite in my mouth, reached for another half sandwich, imagined my buckling up to hang on for a bronco ride of grownups' banter. My mother and I were testimony to the reality that my father was a magician—he could accomplish anything he set his mind on. If he said he could do it, he'd get it done. This we knew. Famous people like Duncan Hines would have said the same thing about him. Walt Disney would have said the same thing about him. He was Big Mike.

My father opened a leather valise and pulled out a *New York Times* newspaper. He paged through it to a dog-eared worn page, folded it backward and held it up for us to see. There was a quarter page advertisement in the top right corner that 19,243,900 subscribers of the *New York Times* on that same day in 1956 could have been holding up and reading at the same time.

PUBLIC AUCTION - MIKE ANTIL ESTATE – DELPHI FALLS, UPSTATE NEW YORK.

"The auctioneer's people will be here in the morning for a walk-through—the barn, the stable, and the house," my father said. "They'll need to get a feel of the inventory. Give them their space, they're good. They handle big estate sales. If we let them do their bidding—keep out of their way—it'll all go well."

I didn't know the details at the time, but my father had spent his and my mother's retirement nest egg and still owed more than $100,000 to creditors who built what amounted to a somewhat defunct—before it even opened—Distelfink Soft Ice Cream stand and diner on what had become a crippled Route 11 highway in North Syracuse. To my older, overeducated siblings, the Distelfink would become the new *dam*—more fodder for their father's log of folly.

I can remember my mother sitting stoically, listening to the man she had been devoted to from the moment they met—had carried, breastfed and lovingly reared eight of his children and would forever stick by the man who had more genuine integrity and drive than any character or hero she'd ever known or read about. She wouldn't second-guess or question his motives during this metamorphic evolution in their life together. My mother had confidence in herself and knew if he needed help, he wouldn't think twice about asking her to step up to the plate. Her steadfast silence was proof of her confidence in herself. I remember being able to see it in her eyes, sitting at the table. She trusted him implicitly.

I sat there imagining '*Am I watching history being made?*' —like was this what it was like being in a desperate war room with General Eisenhower in England while he was planning the D-Day Invasion, or in a tent somewhere with General Ulysses S. Grant planning an assault on Richmond? Or, like the time my basketball team in a championship game at North Syracuse High was in a time out—down seven points and with twenty-seven seconds on the clock. My father's barking of curt, honest, no-nonsense sentences was like Walter Winchell, a radio newscaster we'd listen to during the war.

"What are we selling, Mike?" my mother asked.

"Mommy, my dot on the wall isn't what we're selling. My dot is who do I owe and can I pay them—"

"How many people are coming, Dad?" I asked.

"I don't know, son, but expect all hell to break loose tomorrow and you probably won't be disappointed. There's no way of knowing. Depends on a lot of things—the weather—a lot of things. Just stand back and watch."

"Can somebody loan me money?" I started.

My father reached in his pocket and pulled out a small wad of bills.

"Whatcha' need, son?"

"I want to sell hot dogs, Dad. Maybe Holbrook and I can do it," I said. I was afraid my mother might shut me down on the idea, but she smiled when my father looked at her for approval.

"You going to split it?" my father asked.

"He's my best friend—down the middle," I said.

"Tell you what, son. Go to Hastings' and get hot dogs and buns—don't forget mustard. Put them on our account. It'll be our treat to you and your friend, son. Okay, Mommy?" my father asked.

My mother smiled.

"This will be a good learning experience for you, Jerry," my mother said.

"What'll your hot dogs go for, son?" my father asked.

"I'm thinking fifty cents," I said.

"Son, you're not going to have any competition. People will work up an appetite driving five or six hours from New York City. I'd up the price, ask for more and you might want to maybe think about having them buy a lemonade, too. Whatever you sell the hot dogs for, offer lemonade for another dollar," my father said.

"Dad, if you were doing it, what would hot dogs sell for?"

"I'd say three dollars for both—a dog and a drink, son. Sell them together, a hot dog and lemonade—three dollars."

My mother, the forever teacher, spoke up.

"Don't just tell him how, Mike—teach him why," my mother said.

"Son, people don't like to have to make decisions. You ask them what they want and if they have to think hot dogs and lemonade—which or both—it'll slow your line down to a crawl. If you sell one thing—hot dog and lemonade—three dollars, they just have to stand in line. Other than how many they want, no decisions to make."

My mother smiled.

"Mom, can we cook in the kitchen?" I asked.

"Son," my father said, "the laundry room has a Dutch door to the outside. Why don't you set up the hotplate in the laundry room? Get the biggest soup pot we have and boil the hot dogs—a lot of them at a time. You'll need the tongs. Open the top of the Dutch door and make that your sales counter."

I can remember adrenalin making me stand to ask my mother if I could use her car, and her nodding *yes*—neither of us taking the time to think I only had my six-month learner's permit, which didn't allow me to drive in the daytime without a licensed driver in the car with me and never after dark. I grabbed the car keys off the kitchen counter, ran out to her station wagon and drove to Delphi. Hastings' store was closed for the night, so I walked next door and knocked on his house door. I told Mr. Hastings that Holbrook and I were selling hot dogs, and I asked him if he had a bunch of hot dogs and buns I could pick up in the morning, early.

"How many, son?" Mr. Hastings asked.

"Mr. Hastings, may I use your telephone, please?"

Mr. Hastings pointed at his house phone. I stepped in his living room, picked up the receiver and asked Myrtie, the operator, to ring New Woodstock 78.

My father answered. "Hello?"

"Dad, how many hot dogs should I get?" I asked.

"You with Ralph, son?"

"Yes, sir."

"See if he has a hundred each—dogs and buns, son. You'll need a lot of mustard. Don't forget relish—New Yorkers like their pickle relish. If you need more of anything you can always go back. Don't forget, get plenty of lemons for the lemonade. Get a big bag of sugar."

We hung up.

"Mr. Hastings—" I started.

"I heard him, son. I'll have to make some calls, but I'll have what you need early morning."

"Mr. Hastings, if you could only sell one soda pop in your store, which pop would you pick? What would be the most popular?" I asked.

"If you're talking selling pop, nothing else—no food, I'd go with Coca Cola or Pepsi."

"How about with hot dogs, Mr. Hastings?"

"Probably go with orange pop. Why you asking son?"

"I need a bunch of cases of orange pop, and let's forget about the lemons," I said.

"You'll make more profit mixing and selling lemonade, son," Mr. Hastings said.

"Yeah, I know—but we got sulfur water at the house and the lemonade will taste awful to out-of-towners," I said. "New Yorkers might puke at the smell. It could kill their appetites and our hot dog sales altogether."

"Mind telling me what's going on, son?"

"Mom and Dad are having an auction at our house tomorrow."

I remember Mr. Hastings tweaking his chin, as no one, including the Hastings, had a question about Big Mike and Mary not making good.

"Son, let me get on the phone. I've gotta' wake a few people."

"Okay, thank you Mr. Hastings."

"But come morning I'll have your hot dogs and buns and orange pop."

"Come to the auction and you and the Mrs. get a free hot dog and pop—Marie too," I said.

I left his house and drove up Cook's hill, went through Fabius and turned onto Berry Road to go to Holbrook's house. I knocked on the door. Bob saw it was me and came out.

"What's up?" Bob asked.

"Get in the car. I'll tell you on the way."

"Where to?"

"Our place. You've gotta stay over tonight."

"Hold on, then," Bob said.

He ran up to his room, grabbed another shirt, a comb and underwear, came down and got in the car. When we got to the house my mother told me to pick up my bedroom, dust-mop the floor and put things away. Bob and I went to my room, and he sat on the bed while I started rolling things up—jeans, shirts, T-shirts and socks, one shoe and tossing them on my closet's bottom shelf. Holbrook stood up and nudged me aside.

"Don't be such a slob, Jerry."

He lifted everything out of the closet and set it on the bed. He folded each item and stacked them. In no time my bedroom was spotless. I remember how impressed I was with Bob's patience and his attention to detail. Years later, when I pointed out that moment to him, he explained. "When you were as poor as we were with eleven kids in the house, you learned how to take care of your things."

Bob was definitely a manager. When we went into the laundry room for the first time to set it up for hot dog cooking and sales, he did a turnabout, like he was scoping the room. He ordered me out.

"I'll be the inside man, Jerry. I'll do the cooking and serving. You be the outside man. You get everybody to want a hot dog."

It sounded like a plan. For hours after the crowd began rolling in there were never less than ten people in line waiting to buy hot dogs and pop. I had to run to Hastings' once to buy 50 more hot dogs and buns. I remember my father coming in and telling my mother how surprised he was to see people bidding big money on boxes of spare tools and tires.

"They'll be in the house in maybe half an hour, Mommy," my father said. I remember watching a lady carrying a set of iron Indian Head bookends my mother had from her childhood for her set of Mark Twain books in Minnesota and my having, for the first time that day, a sense that the auction was more than furniture and fixtures. It was becoming personal.

I remember feeling violated when watching my guidance counselor carrying the thermos warmer my mother served pancakes in the day before. I remember my mother going to the china cabinet, opening the door with the key in its keyhole and lifting a stack of dishes.

"Not the china, Mike."

My father read the eyes of the woman he'd loved from the day they met almost a half century before. He reached in the cabinet, grabbed a tall stack of dishes and nodded for me to grab what I could, and we stacked everything that went with my mother's wedding china pattern on their bed. The auction went on for another hour or two. As it was winding down, my father stepped into the laundry room while Bob was counting our money.

"How'd you do, boys?" my father asked.

"Mr. Antil, how much did the hot dogs and buns cost?" Bob asked.

"Together, maybe twenty cents, son—less," my father said.

"Are we still open?" Bob asked.

I pushed the door closed.

"Everybody's gone. We're closed," I said.

Bob looked at the bills in his hand and did some mental calculations.

"I think we just made 380 dollars," Holbrook said.

He started to count it again, and this time he stacked the bills by denomination. My father smiled and left the laundry room. I remember watching Bob's eyes as he counted.

"Hey, man, what's wrong?" I asked.

Bob didn't respond. It was as if his mind was blank.

"I'll meet you up on the white rock," I said. I carried the hotplate, pot, and tongs into the kitchen. I put the remaining hot dogs, buns, mustard, and relish into the refrigerator. I went out through the front door, kicked my shoes off at the creek bank, crossed the creek and climbed up to the big white rock.

I sat patiently, waiting for Holbrook. When he came up, he sat next to me on the rock and pulled a folded wad of bills from his pocket and held them out.

"You were going to cry down there," I said. "What's up with that?"

"Shut up, I was not," Bob said.

He nudged the bills into my chest.

"Are you okay, man?" I asked.

"I'm okay," Bob said.

"I know that face I saw down there, man. Something's up—what was going on?" I asked.

"Counting the money, something dawned on me, is all," Bob said. "It's no big thing, Jerry."

"You're my best friend."

"You're mine, too."

"So, what dawned on you down there?" I asked.

"What have we been—three, four hours selling hotdogs?" Bob asked. I looked at Bob's wristwatch.

"Three hours and seventeen minutes maybe," I said.

"In three hours and seventeen minutes we made more money than my father makes for a whole month of busting his ass, breaking his back for the railroad," Bob said.

I insisted Bob keep the $380. He didn't want to take it, but from that minute on, regardless of the number of years or miles that would pass between us, we knew we could never forget about that day and our friendship. That memory was the true test of the moment Bob and I knew we would be best friends for life—always in each other's heart—no matter where either of us ended up or what roads we each traveled. In our hearts we knew we would be traveling different highways—no longer an *Outdoor Life* magazine back cover dream of becoming a forest ranger or animal bounty hunter. Bob would go on to use his organizational skills to become the plant manager of 7,000 employees at Carrier Air-Conditioning, Syracuse division. He'd take early retirement and open several successful restaurants.

That auction day in Delphi Falls ended with most of the house furnishings gone, making it look like a pavilion again. The barn was stripped of storage boxes, tools, saddles, and bridles. All the animals were gone. I knew when I saw my father picking up his valise it was another signal. He was getting ready to leave again. Asking him where he was going would have been like guessing where a ball would bounce when jumping for a rebound.

"Jerry, me boy—go fire up the grill, learn the coffee maker. People love the first cup. It's not that hard—you might think about giving regulars free fill-ups. Good luck, son," my father said.

"Are you opening Distelfink, Dad?"

"No son, you are …"

"What?!"

"Maybe Holbrook can help. Looked to me like selling hot dogs gave him a taste of it—ya think, son?"

"How about the ice cream machine?" I asked.

"Let Dick figure that one out. Tell him everything he'll need is in the walk-in cooler. It's pretty easy."

"Are you sure, Dad?" I asked.

"Look in on your mother, son."

"I promise," I said. "I will."

My father extended his hand. I shook it.

"Is the Thruway open?" I asked.

"She's open, son."

"Is Route 11 dead now, like you thought?"

"Maybe not dead, son, but it's bleeding bad."

There was a taxicab coming through the gate and up the drive.

"Where're you going, Dad?" I asked.

"Son, I'm heading out to see what opportunities there are available for me. Might be I'll have to go several places before I land something. Let's not put tacks on a map with disappointments—let me go see what I can find. I've made some friends over the years."

"It's like you're in a boat and going fishing, Dad?"

"That's exactly what it's like, son. You mind the store, I'll find where they're biting."

My father took my mother by the hand and they walked like schoolkids out to a waiting taxicab. They embraced and kissed. He got in the taxi and it drove away with my mother standing there, watching the road dust billow behind the taxicab as it passed through the gate and headed to the Syracuse airport.

That was June 1957. It wouldn't be until the third week in November when I would learn where my father had gone off to. I didn't know it yet, but from that June day until the third week in November I was about to live on a cot on the unfinished second floor of Distelfink restaurant in North Syracuse. My mother had to stay at Delphi Falls to button up loose ends.

Chapter 27

"The true test of a man's character is what he does when no one is watching." ~ John Wooden

I was 16 and had never been away from my family longer than the two nights I stayed up at Paul Smith College the year before. I was about to spend the summer plus a dozen weeks of the upcoming school year—my senior year—alone, with no one watching over me. My limited awareness of the bigger picture of the day could only let me assume now that my mother had a lot of work to do and was about to spend the summer tying up "loose ends" following the auction. My brother Jim had convinced her he should stay at the house to keep an eye on it and that he'd be able to continue his *Grit* newspaper delivery. My brother Dick disappeared; rumor had it he wanted to reinvent himself.

My driving license was good and I would be taking the Chevrolet station wagon up to Distelfink. My brother Paul and I were standing on the top of what remained of the concrete dam. We were passing time, watching the creek trickle on by around us. Paul pulled handfuls of shale from the cliff and tossed them, trying to make them skip. We'd break the silence, expressing the feeling of abyss we could sense the family was in, and neither one of us was able to predict what was happening or where it would wind us up as a family.

I remember gripping the wooden handle of a pencil-sharp long shoreman's hay bale hook that one of the auctioneers had left behind. My brother Paul was standing near the edge of the dam pontificating, announcing for the first time that he wouldn't be going to Distelfink with me. He had interviewed with the *Syracuse Post Standard* and was taking a job selling advertising and was going to rent a room in Syracuse. I remember suggesting that this was the time our father and mother really needed us and my brother Paul making a disparaging remark about my father's drinking. It was the cold, distant tone in his voice that sparked me to overreact and I pushed him off the dam. He fell eight feet and landed on gravel. He rolled over on his back, sneering. I jumped off the dam and stood over him, my feet straddling his chest. I dropped to my knees putting my face in his. I let the glare in my eyes speak. I added a Captain Hook-like theatrical exclamation by slamming the haybale hook into the ground a foot away from his head—leaving it buried, and stood up.

    I climbed up the creek bank and walked to the station wagon. My suitcase was on the back seat. I got in the car alone and drove away. I remember the emptiness of that hour of driving to North Syracuse. There was a sensation seasoning inside me that, for the first time in my life, I couldn't recognize what I was driving away from, and I didn't know what I was driving toward.

    Brothers could live through moments like Paul and I had just experienced, but that moment was the last I would see of him for a while. He'd never impugn my father's character in my presence again. To this day I don't have a clear understanding of what my mother was doing that summer other than hearing that she was not at the Delphi Falls house a great deal of the time. I can only speculate she was traveling between friends, lawyers, and creditors, saying goodbye and bringing them up to speed. But I can only guess.

At 16, my emotional maturity was more passionate and less forgiving than today, but as I write this, I am that 16-year-old and my siblings weren't there to help. They had their reasons. I considered them excuses.

Fred, a Cornell Hotel School graduate, didn't come to Distelfink to help. He was a Marine lieutenant at Quantico. Mike was married, teaching at North Syracuse High, not far from Distelfink. Mary was married and living in Little Rock, Arkansas. Dorothy was married, living in Forrest City, Arkansas, and teaching at the University of Memphis.

As for Dick, he came to Distelfink, but on his own terms after reinventing himself. He had sold his white 1956 Plymouth convertible, kept the cash and money he saved from his working at EASY Washer and driving cab as "flash cash," as he'd call a roll or wad of cash he carried for "show."

He had trimmed his sideburns, put away his leathers and bought a used, spotless, deep-green luxury four-door Chrysler Crown Imperial. It looked like a limousine. Dick had two new friends, his cohorts, John and Darryl. They were guys he had met in a Syracuse night. Among the three of them, after Distelfink closed for the day, they would take turns driving the Crown Imperial and roam the city's nights like pimps. He and his two friends never did drugs or marijuana. Their toke was living the "finer life"—a big expensive car and flashing a wad of cash.

In a sense, Dick was patterning his nightlife after the lifestyle of that wealthy town drunk my mother threw out of the house. The only difference was Dick and his two pals stayed sober. To keep up their new image they each had custom-tailored slacks and coats made. Dick had two expensive cashmere sweaters, two pairs of flannel slacks, and Bostonian shoes. Their high was smoking cigarettes while sitting in the comfort of plush velvet car seats, pointing out the window at people and gnarly nighttime city scenes while telling stories to each other.

It would be in the wee hours of the morning when their night would end and the Chrysler Crown Imperial would slowly approach the front of Distelfink, like a feral cat on the prowl. It would stop and idle until a rear door opened and Dick got out. He'd walk to the front door of Distelfink, and the car would quietly disappear—to be washed and waxed, vacuumed out, and parked to wait for the next all-night tour.

Dick would pull on a gold keychain attached to his beltloop, unlock the front door, let himself in and lock it behind him. In the dark he'd go to the cash register like a night watchman doing his rounds, open the drawer, take out a few bills—never all the bills—and fold them around his flash wad. He'd go to the men's room, leave the door open and relieve himself. He'd climb the stairs, undress and put his pressed flannel trousers on a tailor's varnished wooden hanger and hang them on a rope clothesline hung above his cot that was by the wall furthest from the stairs.

For all intents and purposes, I was living alone, sleeping on a cot under a bay window that still missed a glass pane between stacks of lumber resting on two sawhorses over the Distelfink soft ice cream stand and diner. I was using one of the four cots I had commandeered. A small suitcase was my wardrobe and bureau. A wind-up alarm clock would wake me before dawn and I'd pull on khakis, a T-shirt, and head downstairs in the dark to brush my teeth in the men's room. Still in the dark but now with the night lights of a cold city filtering in through the front glass wall, I'd fire up the grill.

I'd open two pounds of bacon and set a dozen eggs on the shelf next to a can of shortening. While the grill heated, I'd put a pound of butter into a stainless-steel container and set it nearby so the butter would soften for the toast. I'd go in the back room, turn the kitchen light on for the first time and see to it the coffeemaker was filled with freshly ground coffee and brewing, and that the milk dispenser had a full can of milk in it, chilling.

My insecurities were comforted—perhaps masked is a better word—by my anal-retentive morning rituals at Distelfink until, like clockwork, there'd come a rapping on the front door that would announce my friends Tony and Carlo, the Italian brothers from Brooklyn who each owned dump trucks. They would come to Distelfink for breakfast and coffee every morning before driving their rigs to construction sites to haul loads of dirt all day at $125 a load.

    I would go to the door, unlock it, look out in the dawn with a sigh, admire their enormous trucks, both washed and polished. I found comfort in seeing Tony's and Carlo's morning smiles. They were my signal all was good, and I'd be safe unlocking the doors in the big city at this early hour. I'd hold the door for them, and then I'd go back into the kitchen to switch on the interior restaurant lights and the Distelfink road sign. It was another day and Distelfink was open for business.

    It was a "learn as I go" summer for me. I had no books for running a diner, or even a serving counter. There were no rules for soft ice cream sales. Distelfink didn't have a menu. I asked Holbrook to go to a few places, snoop out what kind of sandwiches I should be making, find out what was in them and how much I should charge for them. I remember going to a grocery store on Route 11 and buying three pounds of ground beef and some hamburger buns in case someone wanted a hamburger or cheeseburger. I would spend an hour every day slicing a few tomatoes, a few onions, and pressing hamburger patties with a gadget on the butcher table in the kitchen. I'd separate the patties with wax paper and cover everything with clean kitchen towels and put them in the walk-in cooler.

    I used the trick my father taught me at the auction—people not liking having to make decisions. If someone came into Distelfink, I'd approach them with empty cups and a fresh pot of coffee. I'd set cups on the counter and suggest an egg sandwich on white with mayo or, *"How about a BLT with mayo?"* One of the more popular requests was grilled cheese, and I remember staying up all night and burning through two loaves of white bread trying to figure out how to make grilled cheese sandwiches. That night taught me three things. One, it wasn't the amount of cheese I used that mattered, it was the salty flavor of melted cheese when biting into it that made the moment. A thinner slice of cheese worked for that. And two, a medium-heated grill was best for cooking. The medium heat was more moderate and wouldn't burn butter, and butter was the best for letting eggs soft cook themselves and for bringing the white bread of a grilled cheese sandwich to a perfect golden brown while melting the cheese inside. I'd garnish plates with a pickle.

The third thing I learned was that I could do anything if I only tried. Customers would come in groups. There would either be a dozen people at the counter for a half hour or so through breakfast or lunch or none for the few hours in between.

One day Dick brought a girl into Distelfink. He had talked her into working as a carhop waitress for tips. After we'd close up for the day, Dick would hint for me to go upstairs and not come down without asking if the coast was clear. He and the carhop girl weren't quiet about their partying in the kitchen. I remember being curious about the salacious giggling below me. Dick would eventually come upstairs, change into slacks, dress shoes, and shirt, pull on a cashmere sweater, offer a salute and leave. When it got quiet downstairs, I knew the Chrysler Crown Imperial had most likely pulled in for Dick and he and his friends were off for the night, driving the city.

One still dark early morning he came upstairs and woke me. He rested a Webster Chicago wire recorder and a portable record player on the end of my cot. I sat up and rubbed my eyes.

"They invented the wire recorder for General Eisenhower's fake army," Dick said. "This is it."

"What do you mean his fake army?" I asked.

"This machine let Ike's guys play loud recordings of tanks moving about all night to scare off German spies."

"Why'd they do that?" I asked.

"Ike wanted Hitler to think the Allies were going to land in Calais and not in Normandy. It was a ruse—his fake army," Dick said.

He plugged the wire recorder in and turned it on. A groaning and moaning of a man and a woman apparently having sex filled the room. Dick got the wire recorder from an after-hours Army-Navy store in Syracuse after he got the porno that he had traded three packs of cigarettes for in an alley near a brothel off East Genesee Street.

"What's with the record player?" I asked.

"I've got the original recording of Benny Goodman's *Sing Sing Sing* at Carnegie Hall—the whole thing. It takes both sides of the record," Dick said. "Wait 'til you hear the drummer Gene Krupa steal the show—they went wild."

I remember sitting there, becoming cognizant for the first time. I was witnessing my brother Dick, almost as if he was a sculpture, carving his own persona before my eyes. It was as though he knew one day I would be a writer and he wanted me to paint an accurate portrait of him.

Dick stood at the end of my sleeping cot in his gray flannel slacks and his charcoal gray cashmere sweater, presenting his provenance—the historic wire recorder and a porno he earned via a side alley of verbal finessing and bargain banter worth listening about over drinks sometime. Watching him tell how he got the porno was like he was on stage and cheating a character in a play. It was as if he was streetwise enough to know that storytelling was how I could best deal with it and not be looking down at him or his friends.

I remember my Distelfink conundrum in the empty moments, feeling good about what I was learning on my own, watching customers smile after biting into something I prepared. At the same time, without my mother around, my being away from Delphi Falls and alone every night, I'd never forget the pit in my stomach. It was a hollow feeling that would eventually lead to my having ulcers.

Holbrook would come out to see me. One time he gave me a single barrel, 12-gauge shotgun and a box of shells in case I saw a pheasant in the tree nursery's wooded acres behind the Distelfink. We'd play the jukebox and pinball machine. That was the summer the small, handheld transistor radio first came out, and I bought him one. He and I would sit at the counter drinking coffee like we were customers, and he'd never ask if I was coming back to Fabius my senior year. He didn't want to risk depressing me.

I remember the morning the two brothers from Brooklyn came to the front door and my noticing only one of their dump trucks was parked in front. Tony's dump truck was not there. He had hosed down his truck that morning. He climbed up in the cab to come to Distelfink for breakfast and forgot to lower the open-box bed in back. When he drove it under a bridge on Route 11, the towering open-box bed slammed against an overpass, destroying his truck and any chance of it earning him a living until it was repaired. The brothers had to go back to Brooklyn and came to say goodbye. I gave them free breakfast and coffee—Tony for losing his truck, and his brother for standing by his little brother. There was melancholy in the moment, seeing an end to someone who made an impression on me. It was like Tony, Carlo, and I were ships passing in the night—and that morning was the end to a chapter in my life.

My oldest brother, Mike, taught chemistry at North Syracuse High. He had come to Distelfink to tell me I was to go to North Syracuse high school that fall. Those were my mother's orders, and I could use the station wagon to drive myself there. I was about to go to a school with 2,000 strangers. I wouldn't be with the friends I grew up with in kindergarten through 11th grade in Fabius. I remember how alone I felt at the time. Was it the time in my life when I was supposed to leave home, like Paul, and find my own way?

I can remember having a sense of growing up—maturing—the time Holbrook talked me into climbing up on the roof of the Distelfink so we could watch the stars and see if we could see the movie screen of the drive-in movie across Route 11. I remember sitting up there, hearing the crickets and croakers from the garden nursery in the back and listening to Bob talk about not being sure where his life would take him after he graduated the following year. As I look back, I remember witnessing siblings like Holbrook and my friend Johnny Cook in very large, poor families having innate senses of responsibility that would keep them at home longer than usual just to pitch in and help out.

I remember my feeling, for the first time, that maybe it was time I grew up and took control of my own life—and maybe our sitting on the roof of Distelfink was a sign—kind of like when I used to sit on the white rock and think I could read signs of life down below.

Chapter 28

"But this enterprise on which I'm about to embark is fraught with eminent peril." ~ W.C. Fields.

It finally happened—a revelation.

I was scrubbing and rinsing the pots and pans, looking out through the opened back door of Distelfink at the final day's sunset on the nursery's trees. It was promising to be a harvest moonlit night. Dick came in the kitchen and asked me if I wanted to ride with him and the guys— *"get out of this dump, see the real world."*

He had never invited me before. He promised not to be blowing cigarette smoke in my face all night. His smile seemed earnest, and he convinced me to see his world for the first time, with him as my guide and his best friends along in their Chrysler Crown Imperial. He insisted I dress the part, look nice—after all, it was their party I was going to, and first impressions were lasting impressions in their wild kingdom.

He took me upstairs and like a tailor, he pulled things from hangers and boxes. He lent me his gray flannel slacks, unwrapped a new T-shirt and tossed me a charcoal gray cashmere V-neck sweater that was softer than a baby kitten.

From the back seat of their car, I felt special, seeing for the first time their world from its inside, through their eyes, not through my imagination's eye. I was witnessing what the three of them looked at, what they heard and experienced while riding in their wheels, their limousine, late into every night. I caught myself aware of being noticeably impressed by their calm demeanor and their approach, the respect they had for their world and its players in an after-hours city stage play.

They never sped. They'd saunter, taking in every drop of all the sights. I was their VIP guest that night. Darryl and John sat in the front, Dick and I in the back. I remember thinking it was like watching weeds and flowers breaking through concrete or asphalt. I could see night blossoms coming up from under a seedier side of Syracuse, a side I couldn't have imagined, before their car pulled up a few feet away from a glass window on a wood frame door of a brick tenement. With Dick's rear window three feet away from it, the wood door opened back and two prostitutes in lacy satin slips showcasing ample cleavage stood behind the screen door. A madame stood to their side in back. Dick rolled his window down.

"How much?" Dick asked.

"Three dollars," the madame said.

"Used to be two," Dick said.

"Price gone up, honey," the madame said.

"The quality ain't," Dick said. He gestured a nod up to John, signaling him to drive on.

I remember feeling embarrassed about what Dick had said to the madame with the prostitutes standing in their underwear, but I can remember giving him the benefit of the doubt by thinking that maybe he was just trying to be funny, and maybe he wasn't being sarcastic or hurtful in what he said to the lady. Maybe his taking the time to speak to her at all was the night world's code, and it was just a gentle hello to all of them, a "Good to see you, ladies." Maybe just coming by to see them—human eye contact to human eye contact—helped them get through their long, lonely night of waiting to earn money to maybe buy diapers or a few cans of food.

I remember thinking they weren't bad people. They were poor people, trying to get by, and I remember not being ashamed of my brother but learning to respect his world, a world he was comfortable in. To me it was as if, with all he had been through—getting his head shaved that time and dropping out of junior college in Joliet and his feeling he didn't fit in—there was a part of this night world my brother could identify with, that he felt comfortable in. He was a somebody in that world and everyone in the night had each other to help get them through it.

As we turned on a downtown street in front of an expensive glove store, there was a man lying on the sidewalk, crouched in sleep. Dick had John pull the car over. Dick got out, went over to the man and squatted down to talk with him. He came back to the car, got in and signaled for John to drive on. With no fanfare he told us he gave the man a fin for a bottle and half a dub for food.

"Made him promise he'd buy food with it."

"What's a fin?" I asked.

"Five bucks," Dick said.

"What's half a dub?" I asked.

"Dub is double sawbuck—twenty bucks," Dick said. "Half a dub is ten bucks."

I remember being impressed with my no-account brother's compassion for others down on their luck. Dick was an enigma. I remember that moment making him my favorite brother.

Three mornings later, after what seemed to me like two days of endless hours of my feverishly having to scratch my testicles and pubic region, not having a clue as to why, I woke Dick up to tell him I thought I had caught something. His eyes barely opened, he lifted his head off the pillow.

"What's up?" he asked.

"I'm itching like crazy," I said.

"Sounds like crabs," Dick said.

He told me what crabs were—an STD—and where they came from and that I must have caught them from wearing his gray flannel slacks.

"I guess I gave you the wrong pair to wear," he said. "Those should be at the dry cleaners."

He rested his head back on the pillow.

"Crabs?!" I asked. "What the hell are crabs?"

"Bugs. Guys and chicks trade 'em. Shave your nuts," Dick said as he rolled over and covered his head with the blanket.

I wanted to slug him but instead, in a panic, I tossed his gray flannel slacks, my cot sheet, my pillow, my blanket, my T-shirt, my underwear and socks out through the glassless window to the ground below and went downstairs naked, two steps at a time into the kitchen to look for a spray can of DDT insect killer. I grabbed it and went out the back door behind Distelfink, naked, and liberally sprayed my crotch, my ass, stomach, armpits, and my legs. The relief was immediate and noticeable. The DDT and a backyard hosing ended my saga with the pubic lice from my brother Dick's secret world.

Later that day when I closed the Distelfink I stood and watched the fog from over Oneida Lake coming in as I locked up. Our carhop drove up to the door and got out of her car all dressed up. She was going to ride with Dick, John, and Darryl that evening. I let her in and locked the door behind her. I stood there watching the moon and stars being smothered by a heavy blanket of fog coming so low I felt I could have reached and touched it.

I can't describe what came over me at that moment with total clarity, but something did, and I rushed upstairs. Dick was standing in his underwear, pulling on a T-shirt while the carhop sat on his cot, watching. I grabbed the shotgun Holbrook gave me, put two shells in my pocket, went downstairs and left through the backdoor of Distelfink.

The roads were light on traffic and I drove to a shore's inlet on Oneida Lake, where I knew there were rowboat rentals. I put two dollars in the honor can, stepped in a boat with a dry floor and began rowing it out. The layer of fog was like a smokey white, like shag rug carpet eight feet over my head. It gave me a virtual sense of being in my favorite book at the time, *The Old Man and the Sea*.

I remember the loneliness of rowing the boat with my Coleman lantern with its cold white light letting me watch the shadow of my oars moving over the water. I remember way off in the distance my hearing what sounded like a heavy flapping of a bird's wings; they were like a steady and repetitive hand clap with leather gloves—*flop, flop, flop*— and I could tell it was a large bird. *"Turkeys are good fliers,"* I said to myself. It could have been a turkey lost in the fog, I thought. Maybe it was a goose or a duck, but they fly in flocks, not alone. Whatever it was, I could tell it was alone and coming in my direction. I stopped rowing and picked up the shotgun. I put a shell in the chamber, cocked it by locking the barrel up. Resting my elbow on my knee, I took a steady aim at the flapping sound and waited. The split second I saw the goose's head and beak break through the cloud of fog I pulled the trigger. The shotgun exploded and the goose dropped immediately down next to my boat. I stared at it floating, feeling bad about shooting it.

I reached down and picked it up by the neck. I held it up, taking in its beauty, its thick coat of feathers and shades of gray colors. I imagined the miles it had traveled each year, the places and things it had seen. I set the goose on the bench in front of me, followed the light on shore with my eye and rowed to the boat rental place.

As I was driving, after replaying through my mind several times the goose coming through the cloud of fog and my seeing it drop instantly, that something flashed through my brain and told me that I knew what I had to do. Maybe it was a sign. It was as if the goose was sent by a bigger force to give me a message.

I drove to Distelfink and parked in the back. In the kitchen I turned the light on and held the goose up. I couldn't see a scratch on its body, no wounds or blood from shotgun pellets. I thought of how quickly it had dropped in front of me. Had it had a heart attack from hearing the shotgun blast? I laid the goose on the butcher table. It had become my metaphor. Not for my being where I was, but maybe for being where I shouldn't be. As quickly as my mind was spinning, I pulled four feet of paper from the roll of wrapping paper and ripped it off. I pulled another four feet and ripped it off. I found black masking tape and patterned large block letters CLOSED on the two sheets and taped them to the front doors. I walked out to Route 11 to be certain they could be read from the highway. I walked back, locked the doors, went in the kitchen and turned the restaurant's interior lights and the Distelfink road sign off for the last time under my watch.

    I remember sitting on a stool at the counter in the dark with a cup of coffee and a Silex pot with more coffee, Patti Page singing *Red Sails in the Sunset* on the jukebox. Then a Hank Williams record came on.

    Hear that lonesome whippoorwill
    He sounds too blue to fly
    The midnight train is whining low
    I'm so lonesome I could cry.

    I don't remember tears. I don't remember guilt about quitting and letting my father down. I do remember a feeling of being on a tightrope between having learned a lot just having to think through things and experiment on my own, in the kitchen—in meeting and talking to people. I felt hollow inside not knowing how long I would have to live above Distelfink, feeling alone, like I had spent an entire summer climbing up a one-way ladder and was on the top rung with no place to go. I listened to Hank Williams in the darkness of the moment singing about the silence of a falling star, and I remembered sitting on the rowboat on Oneida Lake watching the goose coming through the fog—and how that one bird on a planet of billions of birds would live in my memory.

Chapter 29

"Give him an evasive answer. Tell him to go fuck himself." ~ W.C. Fields

North Syracuse High, with more than 2,000 students in 1957, was ten times larger than the entire kindergarten through 12th grade Fabius Central School I had grown up in from second grade through the 11th grade. The only thing I knew about North Syracuse High was that my Fabius varsity basketball team played them in the divisional finals the year before at the school. We led them by seven points for most of the game, but we lost after having four baskets called back for walking, costing us eight points.

I was a bit disoriented because I wasn't going to school with my brother Jim. He was still at Delphi Falls with my mother. I already had a bad taste in my mouth about North Syracuse, but on my first day at school I was intimidated just driving into their student parking lot. It was like I was in another country. I had to find a spot among hundreds of cars, pickup trucks, and motorcycles. I went to the vice principal's office to ask where I was supposed to go.

After my first day, I remember going outside and standing among a gathering of onlookers in the parking lot and watching a fistfight. It wasn't just arm punching and hammerlock wrestling neck holds; this was cold, merciless, bare-fisted knuckles punching on broken, bloody noses, chipped teeth, and cut faces.

The first week alone I saw four fistfights involving eight different guys. Other than in the movies, I had never seen a fistfight—deliberate punching in the face fights—in all my years at Fabius. I'd back away from the crowd, fearful someone might pick a fight with me because of my height or for being a new kid or something.

I remember thinking if I did have to fight somebody, I'd grab a rock in my fist to win it, and I wouldn't hesitate. A broken tooth, or a broken skull—all the same to me. My survival training came early, listening to how President Truman ended the second World War in the Pacific by dropping the second big bomb. The emperor of Japan said no to their giving up and ending the war after the first bomb. So, President Truman dropped another one, and would have dropped a third if he had to.

I remember those thoughts in my head as I looked for my car in the parking lot. If you can't talk them out of it or run away, then win. I found myself in a new culture, and I was beginning to understand why city kids formed gangs or might belong to them. It was to protect each other. In a school with a student population larger than most villages or towns in upstate New York, there was a cold anonymity among students. Walking the halls was like walking the streets in Manhattan. I didn't know who I was anymore. A girl came over to my car and told me she remembered me from Distelfink. She liked my grilled cheese sandwich. She pointed at a car behind her.

"That's my wreck over there," she said.

THE BOY AND THE BIG WHITE ROCK

It was an old Studebaker that needed painting. We talked and the next day she and her friends started coming to Distelfink to pick me up and drive me to school. One morning I was told on the wall speaker to go to the vice principal's office. I thought I was in trouble, but she wanted to tell me that the basketball coach asked if I might stop by his office.

"What for?" I asked.

"He remembers you, Jerry. He wants to get acquainted, welcome you to North Syracuse," the vice principal said.

"Why didn't he call me?" I asked.

"We do have protocol," the vice principal said.

"Is that all?" I asked.

"Is what all, Jerry?" the vice principal asked.

"Can I go?"

"You may be excused."

She handed me a hall walking pass. I got up and left.

Once in a while my friends in the Studebaker would come to Distelfink after they had dinner at home. They'd drive around back and honk. We'd get in our station wagon and go across Route 11 into the drive-in movie, buy popcorn to share and sit cross-legged on the hood and roof, watching the movie and cartoons. I taped red reflective NS9 on the rear window of our station wagon. My eight Studebaker friends and I—girls and guys—became the NS9 gang (North Syracuse 9). The moniker didn't require much thought or invention. It was inspired by a local car dealer's commercial, calling our station wagon model a nine-passenger vehicle. My friends were eight. It just worked out.

The time was passing by, Halloween approaching. I stopped checking the calendar for lack of interest, but my new friends reminded me. Dick never reopened Distelfink, but he continued to live there with me. He, John, and Darryl were steadfast with their nightly comings and goings and their city vigils, and Dick worked an early swing shift on the production line at EASY Washer.

A day before a big North Syracuse High football game, we were standing on the opponent's football field in the dark pitch of Halloween the night before the big game. The football field was on top of an embankment. NS9—my eight companions and I—had jumped in my mother's station wagon with two five-gallon cans of gasoline, a gallon can of house paint, and three brushes, and headed off to the opposition's football field. Some climbed a ladder and painted in large letters *"N S WINS"* on the face of the scoreboard. I helped pour gigantic letters *"N S WINS"* spanning the width of the football field with the gasoline. We gathered, stood back, threw six lighted matches and watched every letter combust into a burst of fiery flames that lit up the night. I remember the football field aglow and immediately hearing a crackling voice shouting.

"Stop, in the name of the law!"

We stood motionless and looked over to see a lone uniformed policeman climbing onto the field, his gun raised. The flames reflected off his badge, buttons, and a shield on his cap. Our standing there, dumbfounded, apparently wasn't good enough for the officer. He raised his arm, pointed his gun in the air, and pumped out four loud gunshots.

Pow! Pow! Pow! Pow!

We froze. He lowered his gun and threatened.

"Hands in the air, everybody!"

I remember a sense that came over us that this guy was crazy. But he was also dangerous. Best we not move a muscle. He treated us like we were the Brinks truck robbers. We obliged without hesitation and were loaded into a paddy wagon and taken into custody. Parents were called by the police chief and told what we were caught doing and that there could be criminal consequences if the school chose to press charges. The police made us swear on a Bible the numbers we gave them were our phone numbers. In my case there was no answer from the phone number I gave them because it was the payphone on a wall next to the pinball machine at Distelfink. I hadn't mentioned that detail. It was my car that we came in, so the police let me drive home on the condition I report to the vice principal's office first thing Monday morning. Everyone else had to wait for their parents to come and get them.

On Monday morning I went directly from the parking lot to the vice principal's office and waited. When I was sent into her office, she stood, solemn-faced, behind her desk.

"Lying under oath is a serious crime," she said.

I thought it best to remain quiet.

"Perhaps you can explain your giving the police a number that wasn't your parent's number—pledging under oath that it was."

"I didn't lie."

The vice principal held up a three-by-five index card.

"I have your number here. The number you gave the police was not this number."

"I don't live at home."

"Excuse me?"

"I gave them the phone number where I live. My father had the phone put in. It's my father's phone. I didn't lie."

"Are you saying your parents don't live with you?"

I didn't respond.

"Have you visited the coach?"

I didn't respond.

"Jerry, there was considerable damage to an expensive new scoreboard. Unless you take responsibility and agree to help pay for it, there will be consequences," the vice principal said.

"Can I go now?" I asked.

"Are you accepting responsibility, Jerry?"

"Yes, I did it. Can I go?"

"I'll need your parents to sign an admission of responsibility, so this can remain a civil matter."

"Can my brother sign it?" I asked.

"Who's your brother?"

"He teaches here?"

"Mr. Antil is your brother?"

"Yes."

"Mrs. Antil is on Line One," the secretary said.

"Wait outside my office, Jerry."

I was leaning on a wall by the door when the secretary told me to go back into the vice principal's office.

"Do you need gas money?" the vice principal asked.

"What?"

"For your car, do you have money for gas?"

"Tank's full."

"I spoke with your mother. Go to your locker, get your belongings. You're to drive from here to Delphi Falls."

"Now?"

"Now. Your parents have agreed to make reparation for your part in the vandalism. You may be excused."

I turned and left the vice principal's office and went to the station wagon without going to my locker. I drove out of the parking lot, happy to see the school in my rearview mirror. It was after I came to a red light in Manlius near the swan pond, waiting to turn left, I remember thinking of North Syracuse High like a nightmare. There wasn't a moment of my experience there that seemed normal or wholesome. I wasn't myself, and I had to find myself again. I remember thinking that in all the time I went there I never once saw my brother. Other than my friends' happy smiles, their comfortable old Studebaker, I had no other memories about attending, sitting in any classes or walking the halls of North Syracuse High, and I was there more than two months.

As I drove through the village of Delphi Falls, the streets were empty. When I turned right at Maxwell's corner my throat started to get dry. I drove up Cardner Road and turned in our driveway. I was finally home, at the falls, after almost half a year. I parked in front of the swings, got out and just stood there, taking everything in. I could see through the house. The large picture windows had no drapes anymore. My mother came out of the house smiling, with a tablet in her hand and a pen. With a big grin she gave me a welcoming bear hug, kissed me on each cheek, my forehead, and then stood back and tall in front of me. With a pointed index finger, she tapped on the middle of my forehead.

"My sons do not prevaricate," my mother said.

I stood there and took it.

"My sons do not disrespect authority," my mother said.

She tapped two taps on my forehead.

"My sons respect a person's property," she added with a final tap on my forehead. She handed me the pad and pen.

"I love you … now go write two "To whom it may concern" apology letters. One to North Syracuse High School for dishonoring their good name. Then you're to write a "To whom it may concern" apology to their host school, where you willfully damaged their property."

"Now?" I asked.

"You have an hour."

I took the pad and pen.

"Where's Richard?" my mother asked.

"I think he's working at EASY Washer again," I said.

My mother hugged me, kissed me on the cheek, turned and walked to the house. I went and sat on a swing seat and took off my shoes and socks. I stood up, set them on the seat, rolled up my pant legs and went behind the barn, looking up at my destination, the big white rock up on the cliff. I tucked the tablet under my belt, the pen in my pocket, crossed the creek barefoot, and climbed the cliff to sit on my favorite meditation ottoman and friend, the big white rock.

I wrote both apologies sitting on it, read them aloud to myself, and tore one up to rewrite without the venom I had poisoned it with about the North Syracuse basketball coach.

I sat on the rock for several hours, apologies in hand, taking everything in below. As time passed, I thought of the horses that weren't there anymore and of Ginger, our dog, who would normally be sitting at my side on the white rock. Ginger was nowhere to be seen. The front and back yards of the house were overgrown. For years, their mowing had been by grazing of two horses, a Shetland pony and a Karakul lamb. I knew Paul had moved to Syracuse and was living in a room there, selling advertising for the newspaper. I remember wondering where my younger brother Jim was.

Looking down at the front gate, it was a complete surprise seeing a deep-green Chrysler Crown Imperial turn in and drive to the house. It was Dick. I tucked the pad under my belt, climbed off the white rock and butt-slid down the grassy portion of the cliff to the creek below. I crossed it, climbed the embankment, and ran over to the Chrysler. Dick and his friends, John and Darryl, were leaning on it. Dick was in the work coveralls he wore at EASY Washer.

"Mom found you," I said.

Mother came out with arms wide to welcome her son, Richard. She hugged him with one arm and me with her other arm. She was a happy mother again. It had been nearly five months. She introduced herself to John and Darryl and welcomed them to Delphi Falls. Forever the manager, she went into a management role and took charge.

"Dick, I need you to wrap your wonderful brains around a problem. I need to get something figured out."

"You do?" Dick asked. His face beamed at being looked up to, being worthy, not a bum. It was in his face.

"A few things—can your friends help?" she asked.

"Anything, Mrs. Antil. You just name it," John said.

I handed her my two apologies. She held them in a tight grip for a later read and began giving instructions.

"Dick, you're in charge."

Dick smiled.

She pointed at a red, two-wheeled trailer that was parked in the barn garage.

"I need you to have the tires checked—see if they're good."

"Yes ma'am," Dick said.

The trailer wasn't sold at the auction—and for a reason, it turned out. My father originally bought it to put a tent on top to haul to ice-fishing lakes. My mother saw the trailer as an opportunity, and the auctioneer bypassed it.

"Dick, I need you to figure out how to pack books and china in the trailer so nothing gets broken or damaged or rained on. You think you can do that, son?"

"Done," Dick said.

My mother had a collection of nearly 2,000 books.

"All the books in the front room—none of the magazines or National Geographics, son. I need everything packed into the trailer. Please be careful. I know you can figure a way to cover them with canvas tarps or something."

"Where are we moving them to, Mom?" Dick asked.

That fell on deaf ears.

"Dick, drive the station wagon into Manlius and buy a trailer hitch somewhere, get them to attach it. We need it to pull the trailer filled with books and china."

"Where we taking them to, Mom?" Dick asked.

"Milwaukee."

"Milwaukee?"

"Milwaukee," my mother said. "You and your friends check to see that it has good tires. Maybe check the oil and water on the station wagon."

"Where're we going, Mom?" I asked.

Dick interceded.

"Milwaukee—it's in Wisconsin, north of Chicago. It's famous for beer and the Milwaukee Braves," Dick said. Dick flagged John and Darryl to follow him to the barn garage.

"Is that where Dad is, Mom? Milwaukee?" I asked.

"Your father's in Milwaukee, son. We don't have time to stand around talking."

My mother raised her voice to be heard in the barn garage.

"Richard?"

"What is it, Mother?" Dick asked.

"John and Darryl are welcome to come with us."

"Where to?" Dick asked.

"Milwaukee."

"When are we going?" I asked.

"Go help your brother, Jerry. Do what he asks. Help him with the books and china. If everything is packed and safe, we can leave first thing in the morning."

"Where's Jim?" I asked.

"He's in school. He'll be home later."

Mother went in the house. I went in the barn garage. Dick and the guys had the trailer jacked up and were checking its tires. We were walking to the station wagon to take it into Manlius for a trailer hitch when my mother came out of the house dressed up like she was going to church. She was walking toward my father's Oldsmobile.

"I'm off to say goodbye to someone. I'll be back."

THE BOY AND THE BIG WHITE ROCK

We didn't learn until later that my mother had met a Stigmata, a Christian mystic, who lived somewhere between Delphi and Cortland. The woman had open sores on her palms, as did the crucified Jesus Christ on the cross. My mother would sit with the lady Stigmata and they would pray together. I remember my mother being open, talking about the lady with the Stigmata and our never questioning her beliefs in the Stigmata lady or her spirituality, nor did my father ever not support her beliefs. Mother told me that when her time came, she wanted to be cloaked with a shroud in her casket, like a nun—and that she believed heaven was a big library.

Jim had grown. That evening we slept on mattresses on the floor somewhere in the house. My mother slept on a mattress on the floor in hers and my father's bedroom. I woke early and climbed the cliff one last time and sat on the white rock, just to say goodbye forever to my memories on it, and to my short lifetime at Delphi Falls. I remember thinking if I let the sights below soak in, they would never leave my soul. For breakfast we stood in the kitchen with individual cans of grapefruit sections and plastic spoons. We tossed the empty tin cans and the spoons into the trash barrel outside. Everyone lined up and climbed into assigned cars. We were going to drive tandem all the way to Milwaukee. Dick would be behind the wheel of the station wagon, pulling the trailer filled with books and mother's china. My mother and Jim would ride with him. John, Darryl, and I were in the Chrysler Crown Imperial following behind. We left my father's Oldsmobile sitting behind the swings. I didn't ask why.

I remember passing through the gate and out onto Cardner Road for the very last time. I didn't feel melancholy driving away from the home I had grown up in. I remember being exhilarated by a feeling of hope—the best I could ask for after the past five months—a hope that we were maybe leaving dysfunction and thoughts of a broken household, and we were coming back together again as a family.

Chapter 30

"We were now about to penetrate a country at least two thousand miles in width, on which the foot of civilized man had never trod." ~ William Clark

I can't speak for my brother Jim in the car ahead of us but to me, a 16-year-old, an all-day car ride in 1957 was just a few steps up from riding in a horse-drawn stagecoach. There was no air conditioning. In the cold, the car's heater would only warm legs of passengers in the front seat. In the 1950s there were no electronic games, no internet or cell phones to while away the time. If you were lucky, you had a pad of paper and pencil and could draw things. My favorite was drawing B-17 bombers flying over Germany I watched in the war on Saturday morning picture show movie newsreels dropping bombs. I'd draw them and the enemy spitfires attacking me with a *rat-a-tat-tat* of bullets streaking through the air. Every car window had to be open for fresh air and wind noises at 60 mph could be deafening.

The riders in our two-car, cross-country caravan were held in the dark as to where we were going next. I was delightfully surprised when we crossed over into Canada and drove to downtown Niagara Falls on the Canadian side. For me, it was always fun in Canada. My father used to cross the bridge in Ogdensburg on occasion and take me to a Mass in Canada so I could experience the sermons in French.

My mother had us park on the street in downtown Niagara Falls. We got out to stretch our legs and wait for her instructions. Hearing the sounds of the loud rumbling of the falls in the background for the first time and seeing its enormous size, with the billowing mists rising from the boulders it splashed down, was awesome. My mother told us she was getting a room for the night at a tourist home, encouraged us to explore, take everything in—see the falls, visit the museums and shops.

She gave us each a dollar. She asked Dick, Darryl, and John to take turns staying with the trailer and protecting it. She announced that our trip to Milwaukee was going to be a learning experience. Niagara Falls was a good start in our adventure. Reading the fronts of postcards for sale was a learning experience. It was an inexpensive way to learn about an area, its myths and legends. In various shops we learned about the daredevils who rode barrels over the falls and their fates; we learned about the oddities in Ripley's Believe it or Not Museum, and, standing by the handrail overlooking the enormous Horseshoe Falls, we met Amish people and Pennsylvania Dutch people in their native dress and straw hats. It was fun listening to Dick talking with them and asking about their habits and beliefs. He told them about the Distelfink—the word being an Amish (German) word for goldfinch—and they smiled.

That night my mother, Jim, and I slept in a tourist home room—me on the floor. Dick, John, and Darryl slept in the cars, taking turns guarding the trailer. It was just after twelve the next day when we finished off our sandwiches and departed Niagara Falls. We made our way through Canada toward Windsor—another surprise. It was fun seeing the speed signs in meters-per-hour and not miles-per-hour. The sun was bright in our eyes when we were crossing west on the bridge from Windsor into the United States and Detroit. My mother used a folded-up map she bought at a gas station and directed Dick to a motel near what was a large historical museum campus called Greenfield Village.

The next day we got to ride on horse drawn carriages and got to see Henry Ford's first house and hear the story about where he built his first Henry Ford Model T engine. He built it in the basement of his house. He couldn't get the motor out through the door, so they had to remove some of the basement wall.

In Greenfield Village were several attractions, including a Thomas Edison Museum where people talked about and showed us many of his inventions, including the light bulb and the voice recording machine.

The next day we drove into Chicago. Mother pointed out the tall, famous Wrigley building, where the chewing gum company was headquartered. Dick told us about the times he spent in Chicago when he went to Joliet Junior College, just south of the city. He talked my mother into taking us to Chicago's Chinatown. He and his friends took turns sitting on top of the trailer, protecting the books. I was happy to see nobody in Chinatown was starving, remembering times at our dinner table when we were told to *finish our food. Think of all the starving children in China.*

After Chinatown we went to the Museum of Science and Industry and walked the long halls with our mouths open in wonderment, seeing three-dimensional display windows with moving exhibits behind them. One started out as a dairy country setting with pastures and red barns and grazing livestock, and that revolved in sections into a city of skyscrapers, and that revolved into futuristic buildings with spaceships and flying cars. I climbed down through the hatch inside a captured WWI German U-boat submarine, bumping my head and having to stoop just to stand at the steering wheel, the ceiling was so low inside.

      The road trip from Delphi Falls and the learning stops we made went a long way toward our being able to put our memories of the tornado-like half-year our lives had been through behind us. For me it was a good start. I remember our driving towards the Milwaukee skyline in the distance and not being afraid.

Chapter 31

"The Eagle has landed." ~ Neil Armstrong

I was 16 and in Wisconsin for the second time in my life. Scribbled on a page of a long-lost diary somewhere was a list of the states we had driven through in the summer of 1952, when we went to see our Boma and Bompa and my father's brothers in Minnesota and then to Arkansas and back to Delphi Falls. Wisconsin was one of those states we drove through.

After turning a corner, Dick stuck his long arm out the station wagon's window and with a big sweeping wave, signaled back to us that he was about to pull over. He stopped the station wagon and trailer on Marshall Avenue in a double park next to an empty Buick, a Chevrolet, and a Ford pickup truck, each legally parked at meters. In the distance I could see the sign for the Schroeder Hotel. I knew we must have been somewhere near downtown Milwaukee.

My mother got out of the station wagon and signaled for us to stay in our car. She went into a building.

    There was a polished brass sign on the wall next to the building's brass and glass double doors. The sign read, "MARSHALL HALL Efficiencies." I was to learn a one-room efficiency meant one room that had everything in it, a kitchen, a bathroom, and bed—the bed hanging on its end and coming out of the back of a closet door and folding down. My mother came outside with a congenial looking man with a warm smile on his face. It was Willy, the building's maintenance man, who would become a good friend, teaching us about coping in a city and about city life. Willy was well dressed, with a shirt and tie and wearing a coverall to keep his suit from getting soiled. We figured their walking out was a signal, and we got out of the cars.

"Welcome to Milwaukee," Willy said.

We waved hello.

"What fine-looking young men, Mrs. Antil. Are these all your sons?"

My mother introduced us to Willy and we shook hands. Willy and my mother announced that our mother was the new manager of the apartment building, Marshall Hall. My father had arranged the interview, and my mother got the job.

"My friends call me Willy," Willy said. "I 'speck you'll do the same."

"You know my dad?" I asked.

"I surely do, son. I see that baking man near every day—all hours," Willy said.

I never learned what my mother was paid, but in return for her managing the building, we were also given two free efficiency apartments. My mother, my father, Jim, and I were going to be sleeping on cots in one of the apartments and my mother's books and china would be stored in the other efficiency apartment down the hall, where Dick, John, and Darryl could sleep on cots.

Dick, John, and Darryl spent the afternoon emptying the trailer after many trips on the freight elevator and organizing everything in stacks in their apartment room. They disposed of the trailer somehow and when they came back into Marshall Hall, Willy explained overnight street parking in Milwaukee.

On our first day or two, I shadowed Dick. I'd follow his exploring the various building amenities, nooks and crannies. In the basement there was a laundry room for tenants. There was a television room, perhaps with 50 or 60 seats and a television in front—a 21-inch picture tube.

There were a few stand-out memories gnawing on me my first day or two at Marshall Hall. The big one was that I came from Delphi Falls to Milwaukee with none of my clothes. I had left them all at Distelfink. The second was I discovered my mother hadn't packed my special basketball sectional champ jacket with varsity letter and divisional emblem crest. I had won it in Fabius the year before. My mother came straight out and told me she meant to leave my championship coat behind.

"We don't want to be boastful or showy in a new city, son. It's not polite. Let's do our best to make a good impression," my mother said. "As to school clothes, let's wait for your father to get home. He'll have some ideas."

My mother had a way of explaining things and laying down the law at the same time in such a way that it would be a fool who would argue. I went down the hall to Dick's apartment to borrow underwear and socks. The door was unlocked and I went in and heard Dick's Benny Goodman *Sing Sing Sing* recording from the Carnagie Hall concert. He and John and Darryl were sitting on the floor by a window listening, tapping their toes, clicking fingers to Gene Krupa's drumbeat sounds. The loud music was an interlude to their strategy meeting—an intermission. The three were each holding a full *Milwaukee Journal* newspaper spread open to scan for jobs or other opportunities that might be available to them in Milwaukee. Dick caught my eye and tossed me a green sheet section of the newspaper for me to pass the time.

    The green sheet contained the *Milwaukee Journal*'s comics and other light reading sections. It was printed on green paper. I browsed it, caught up on my comic strip serials, tried a word puzzle and gave up, sat back, leaned against the wall, and watched the guys scan their newspapers as the Benny Goodman record ended. Dick had already earned my confidence while riding with them on that late night ride through their world they shared with me in Syracuse. I had a respect for their empathy toward people, especially the downtrodden, and what made a big impression on me was not only the simplicity of their own personal needs, but that they had a sense of responsibility to earn money to support those needs—to earn the money to pay for their public lifestyle.

    There I was, sitting on the floor in a Milwaukee building near downtown and feeling like it was as if I was witnessing the beginnings of a whole new unwritten chapter in their book. It was almost like I was in a foxhole with them behind enemy lines in France and Dick, John, and Darryl were about to come up with their plan on how they were going to take Paris. They each folded their newspapers neatly, for later reference, and they set them on the floor between their legs. Dick and

John lit cigarettes and everyone faced each other cross-legged on the floor.

"Guys, I gotta be honest," John started. "I'll help you all I can to get you up and running, but I have to go back …"

"What?" Dick asked.

"My ma needs me."

"Darryl?" Dick asked.

"I'm staying," Darryl said.

"Okay, then," Dick said, "so we think twos, not threes. Not a problem."

"How about the wheels?" Darryl asked. They had purchased the car together.

"John gets the Chrysler," Dick said. "He'll need wheels in Syracuse—and to get there too."

He waited for a response.

"Agreed?" Dick asked.

Darryl nodded agreement.

"Thanks, guys," John said.

Dick took charge and picked up the automobile section of the newspaper.

"We'll need wheels too."

He pointed at a listing he had folded his newspaper to.

"Here's a low-mile Caddy."

"Wow. A Caddy?" Darryl asked.

"It's a 1950—one of them Series 62 jobs, four-door. Looks cherry," Dick said.

"How much?" Darryl asked.

"Two hundred and ninety-five dollars."

"How much is there in the bag?" John asked.

The guy's treasury was in a six-by-nine-inch flat satchel bank bag for cash and receipts.

"About nine hundred something," Dick said.

"We've got enough," Darryl said.

"We'll go look at it today," Dick said.

Dick handed the newspaper to John so he could read the advertisement.

"Next item," Dick said. "We don't have to pay rent, so we've got a free ride on that. Let's talk food. Hamburgers are nine cents each at White Castle. Beers are a nickel in Milwaukee. What's that come to? A buck a day each?"

"A buck, yeah—and some for gas," Darryl said.

"So, there are two ways we can make some bread," Dick said. "First, my mother will pay fifteen dollars to paint an apartment when somebody moves out."

"What can that take— a couple hours?" Darryl asked.

"Next," Dick said. "I figured this one out last night—the pay is two cents each to deliver newspapers."

"Deliver newspapers?" Darryl asked. "What the f---?"

"It's not like we'll be on bicycles or jumping on lawns in neighborhoods. Don't sweat the small stuff, Darryl."

"I'm not riding no bicycle to—," Darryl started.

"This building alone could be a hundred apartments. What's that—nine floors on an elevator? That's two bucks a day, 14 bucks a week—in this building alone, just riding the elevator."

"So, are we going to get this building for the newspaper thing, you thinking?" Darryl asked.

"As a base, but we'll get the whole block—piece of cake. Tips alone could be large," Dick said.

"We paint us a couple apartments a week, we're in gravy," Darryl said.

In one 27-minute meeting on the floor by a window, my brother and his friend established themselves as permanent Milwaukee fixtures. They shared proposals and rebuttals and surfaced as self-sufficient, and by noon the next day, they were the proud owners of a 1950 black Cadillac, Series 62 four-door.

When their meeting wound down, I told Dick about my clothes dilemma: I had none. He rummaged through a suitcase and tossed me two packages of new underwear briefs and T-shirts. He offered me a pair of his gray flannels. I turned them down.

When my father came home that afternoon, we all went down to the empty television room for a family meeting. I knew he was with a bakery. He told us how he got to meet all of the Milwaukee Braves players during the World Series, especially home run king Hank Aaron, who was closing in on Babe Ruth's homerun record.

All I knew was that my father was with a bakery in Milwaukee called Sunbeam Bread, just like the bread brand in Homer, New York. I can remember the first few nights at bedtime in the one-room efficiency. I still see the images—my father lying on his cot, winding up an alarm clock, my mother brushing her teeth over the sink built into the stove and range, and my brother Jim asleep on his cot.

It was like there was an unspoken something about living in those moments. I imagined it was like living in a teepee, like Indians. There was a respect of space and quiet. I remember falling asleep the first few nights while doing the math in my head for how many nights of sleeping on a cot until school was over for me. Should I maybe join the Marines when I'm out?

When morning came, my father was always gone. My mother had my brother Jim and me walk with her to Cathedral for Mass that Sunday. She told us that St. John's Cathedral was the school, next to the church where we would start attending the next day. In Mass, the front pew was lined with Dominican nuns. They were teachers. There were Dominican nuns at the school—in black and white habits. As for my lack of clothes dilemma, the Milwaukee stores were closed on Sunday. My father gave me one of his suits, a shirt and tie to wear to school until I could shop. The next morning, my first day at school, I got off the elevator in the lobby and Willy said hello with a big smile, told me how nice I looked.

"Boy, what size shoe you wear?" Willy asked.

"Twelve D," I said. "Why?"

"Hold on, son," Willy said. "Don't go nowhere."

He went around the corner into his apartment and came back out with a polished pair of black, wing-tipped shoes. He held them out for me to take.

"Try these on, Mr. Jerry."

"What?" I asked.

"I can't have my man going about town lookin' all fine in a suit and a styling tie and then be sporting brown shoes. Here, son, put 'em on. Ain't you heard yet, son? Black is beautiful. You need you some black shoes."

Willy's dress shoes fit, and he and I became friends that morning. Those shoes gave me confidence in making a good impression, stepping into a world new to me. I remember Jim's and my approaching the school. I was timid but confident. I can't remember Jim's moment, but I knew he was a forever entrepreneur with his country newspaper and popsicle cart back at Delphi Falls. I knew he'd survive.

The steps up into the building were old city modest, the school building small, like in an old movie. Once we were in a hall, it was as if we both went our own way. The school was called, "The little mission on the east side," but as if Little Orphan Annie's Daddy Warbucks came through for the mission, the school had a brand-new gymnasium. It was donated by a famous celebrity and graduate, the clarinetist and band leader Woody Herman.

A stand-out memory of my first week there was my homeroom. There were 139 seniors—I counted them—gathering and sitting in desks, and in the front of the room, on a small platform, was a desk for our home room teacher. She was a tall nun with an expressive face—Sister John Dominici—and she sat up there in a statuesque pose, one arm stretched over to the side of her desktop. There was a commanding presence about her, but not without a ready smile in her eyes. She scoured the room. I remember my mornings in home room and then getting to sit in the lunchroom with classmates Dennis Mandick, Bob Loreck, and others. Dennis would top off his sandwich with the rest of his orange soda and Hostess Twinkies.

I can't remember the sequence of events—buying school clothes or going to the gymnasium while the team was practicing—but I was suited up, and the coach going out of his way to tell me that his players worked hard to be on the team and that I would have to sit on the bench. He couldn't just put me in because I was tall. Two things kept going through my head. The first was I really didn't care if I played or not—didn't much care if I was on a team. The second thing was, I wondered if I had my championship coat on when I walked into the gym would the coach have been such a jerk, embarrassing me in front of everyone.

Maybe I should get an after-school job—painting apartments for my mother, delivering newspapers for Dick. Something—whatever. I wondered how old I had to be to join the Marines, so I walked downtown and grabbed a leaflet from a rack at the recruiting office.

My mother made me join the basketball team—show sportsmanship, she said, be a part of the school.

Chapter 32

"They are not ours to keep, but to teach how to soar on their own." ~ Author Unknown

I remember my algebra teacher, Sister Mary Agnes, coming every day to watch basketball practice. She would sit on a sideline bleacher with a pad and pencil, scribbling notes. One day during class, Sister Mary Agnes asked me to meet her in the gymnasium after school. It was some holiday eve and there wasn't practice that afternoon.

The gymnasium was dark, save the light coming through a row of windows over the bleachers that spanned the length of the gymnasium. Sister Mary Agnes looked like a penguin standing in the middle of the court. In her long flowing white and black habit, she couldn't have been five-foot-two standing there with a basketball in her hand. She motioned me to come over to her. I did, and she handed me the basketball.

"I want to see you dunk," Sister Mary Agnes said.
"I can't dunk," I said.
"Yes, you can, Jerome."
"I promise you, Sister, I can't dunk."
"Just try. Go ahead and try."

I tried. The best I could do was touch the rim with my fingertips. I came back to center court. Sister Mary Agnes had me stand there while she went over to the wall by the door and turned the gymnasium lights on. She walked back to center court.

"Try again," she said.

I tried, again, and again, and again. I hadn't dunked the ball with any new try, but I could feel more of my hand touching the rim each time I tried. What I didn't see every time I tried was that Sister Mary Agnes would scribble notes or observations into her spiral notepad.

She watched me a few times more and then called me over to her. She lifted a small fabric image of the Blessed Virgin Mary about the size of a postage stamp and pinned it to my shirt. On it read, *My Mother, My Confidence.*

"Jerome, remember this prayer—and this time I want you to jump from farther out."

"What do you mean, Sister?"

"You have a tendency to run way in under the basket and then jump. Try starting your jump from farther out—like maybe from the foul line to start and then closer in until something happens."

Within four tries I was dunking the basketball.

"Good night, Jerome," Sister Mary Agnes said. She held the door for me, turned out the gymnasium lights. She went to the convent and I walked home.

It was a week later when my father was waiting for me in the lobby. He was talking with my mother and Willy when I walked in. Willy came over to me, looking for a handshake.

"Let me shake the hand of the man. You're the man, son," Willy said.

"What's going on?" I asked.

My father handed me the *Milwaukee Journal* newspaper folded open to the sports page.

"Read this, son."

I read it.

Antil Sparks Cathedral's Rise as Basketball Power

Cathedral's basketball stock has jumped and it's not only because the Eagles have speared four straight non-conference games. One other pleasant surprise that comes along once in a coach's lifetime is a big factor. In Coach Ray Heldeman's case it's the acquisition of Jerry Antil. The 6-6 1/2 newcomer arrived in Milwaukee about two weeks ago and enrolled at Cathedral November 22. After two days of practice Antil was used at forward and center and his soft hook shot beat the Cagers in overtime. He also scored 16 points. Not bad for only two days of drills. But wait, there's still more. Friday night, Antil jammed in a dozen baskets, a pair of free throws and speared 26 rebounds off both boards at the expense of Cedarburg. His total output for five quarters of play is 28 field goals, six charity tosses and 45 rebounds. Antil is far from a one-man team. The Eagles' success is due in no small part to the efforts of Dennis Mandick, Ken Kleinhans, Bob Lorreck, and Gordon Michaels. Michaels, who is 6-5, gives the Eagles good height when teamed with Antil. Heldeman's only regret is that the 16-year-old Antil, who was named on Syracuse's all-star team last season, is a senior. At the moment, however, Ray is mighty pleased that Jerry decided to finish high school at Cathedral. ~ Bob Lassanske – **Milwaukee Journal**

I handed the newspaper to my mother.

"Get in my car, son, I want to show you something," my father said. My mother gave me a big hug.

"Keep an open mind," my mother whispered to me. "Hear your father out. We love you."

What I didn't know was my father was driving me to South Milwaukee.

"Son, this is maybe the biggest year of your young life so far. You're a hero on the court, you're a senior with all your life ahead of you."

"What are you saying, Dad? Where're we going?"

"Son, you'll want to have your friends over—you'll want to entertain. A one-room apartment with four cots in it just isn't the place for a senior basketball player to entertain in."

The car pulled in front of a two-story animal hospital. The veterinarian lived over it.

"What's this?" I asked.

My father told me the doctor's name and that I could be his assistant during my spare time in return for an empty bedroom he had upstairs. I would have full use of the place, the kitchen and living room, and I could entertain my friends and enjoy my senior year.

"I'm thinking of joining the Marines, Dad."

"Son, you have plenty of time to think about that. Right now let's get you started with celebrating a big year in your life. Sometimes we can get caught up thinking about the future so much we forget to live today. Catch the Wells Street trolley anytime. It's a block away and it'll take you to school or to come see us."

I did move in with the doctor. He was a short, overweight, distant kind of man, not warm. When he'd come upstairs it was like I wasn't even there. My friends would come over and we would talk or play cards. I could cook pork chops or make grilled cheese sandwiches. In my bedroom I had my personal turn to the wall times, still dumb as a rock regarding the female sex. I would flirt with girls on the telephone. Kenny Kleinhans would bring scissors and trim my hair before games.

Three instances stand out from the animal hospital below where I lived. One was a basset hound that bit the vet and the vet took a broom handle and beat it—only to find out the reason the basset bit him was that its back was broken and he was in pain. On another memory the doc called me downstairs. When I got there, he handed me a large boxer dog to hold in my arms. The dog had blood all over his face and ears. It had been hit by a car. I remember the doc bringing a four- or five-inch needle into the room—told me to hold the dog still. He injected the needle and I'll never forget what it was like to feel that animal die in my arms when I was 16. I actually felt it fall limp.

I was upset because the doc hadn't told me he was going to put the dog down—but I can remember the dog felt lighter when it was alive and heavier when it was dead, and for sure God had something to do with that. My last memory of living with the vet was on Christmas Eve. We had to do an hour surgery on a poodle who was having a litter and one of the pups had broken through her intestine or something. The mother dog died, but we saved four of the puppies.

Our team did well that year. I was put on the All-Star All City league. At the All-Star game, I sat on the bench with Fran Allison, star of the popular *Kukla, Fran and Ollie* television show. She sang "The Star-Spangled Banner" before the All-Star game. I was put in the game in the last 18 seconds. I was invited to the Milwaukee High School All Star Dinner Banquet but I didn't go. From the animal hospital I had called Marquette University in Milwaukee and was told my grades weren't good enough to get in there.

I remember our senior prom and my date, and everyone riding on the Wells Street trolley the night it made its very last ride. I remember the day I went to school, walked into my homeroom and to my desk. Sitting there looking around at the people I had known only for a year, and the good friends I had made among them. I wondered where we would all be a year from now. I remember looking up at Sister John Dominici, sitting like royalty at her desk on the platform. I'll never forget her catching my eye, smiling at me—her getting up and walking over to my desk.

"Seems you've got some admirers, Mr. Antil," Sister John Dominici said. With that, she placed a stack of 18 unopened envelopes on my desk. They were from colleges. I took them to the Marshall Hall and everyone met in the television room-- Mom, Dad, Dick, Jim, and Willy. One by one, my mother read the 18 basketball scholarship offers enclosed in those letters. My mother chose Xavier University for me. It was a Catholic school.

They also had won the NIT that year, but that wasn't a factor in her decision.

Two other memorable things happened that year in Milwaukee. The first was while watching television downstairs with my brother Dick one time, a pretty girl who lived in the building was sitting in the front row. Dick leaned over to me.

"I'm going to marry that girl," Dick said.

It turned out that the girl, Pat, was totally deaf and teaching herself how to speak. She could read lips and could articulate with a broken dialect. Dick knew she sat in the front row in the room to practice reading lips by watching people on television. He always gave her space. It was love at first sight between them and they would each change each other's lives forever—more in the epilogue.

As for my mother and father, there were two things that happened of which I was unaware. One was that after sending all their money earned in Milwaukee back to their creditors for Distelfink, they were nearly paid in full. The second was an old friend in the baking business, Mr. Forks, from Fort Wayne Indiana, invited my father to move to Fort Wayne and become his partner at his Holsum Bread bakery.

And so ended my seven-odd months in Milwaukee, Wisconsin, my senior year of high school.

Epilogue

"The future ain't what it used to be." ~ *Yogi Berra*

As for me and my birds and bees training, my first two serious girlfriends became nuns. One a Maryknoll nun, one a Mercy Order nun.

In 1963, when I was six-foot-ten, it was the dawn of the largest sexual revolution the world had ever seen—the result of the invention of the birth control pill. I was a frustrated 22-year-old and Newport, Kentucky, was an underworld open city of illegal gambling and prostitution.

Two Catholic friends joined me, and we walked across the Cincinnati/Newport toll bridge, paid our penny tolls, and went into a small diner in Newport to plan our strategy on how to lose our virginity. We sat at the counter and asked a waitress in a spotless, heavily-starched white uniform for coffee.

"We don't serve coffee, hon," she said.

She smiled and raised her brow.

"No coffee?" I asked. "What—?"

"Where y'all from, sweetie?"

"Across the river," I said.

I pointed at my two friends.

"They go to X," I said. "I went there too—we won the NIT—we live in Cinci."

The waitress smiled at our being from out of state. That was our passport and ticket in.

"Want girls?" the waitress asked.

With goofy grins we nodded our heads. The wall behind the lady was mirrored. She touched a section of the wall and a door opened.

"First drink's free, boys. Plenty of girls."

In the back room a girl reached around my barstool and grabbed my personals and whispered, "It's eleven dollars to go upstairs, honey." She gave my boys a teasing squeeze. I counted out eleven ones and set them on the bar. She took me by the hand like I was a schoolboy and led me up the steps to the balcony floor and into a room.

I remember a corner sink and her washing it with warm water and Ivory soap as the highlight of her otherwise few minutes of inconvenience ….

But I digress.

My sister Mary graduated Phi Beta Kappa from Syracuse University and had a lifetime career teaching seven years of high school French. She was a published poet.

My sister Dorothy graduated from Syracuse University, was a professor at the University of Memphis and went on to be one of the founding members of the AFSCME, the government employee's union.

My brother Mike taught sciences at North Syracuse High School.

My brother Fred earned his doctorate and became Associate Dean at Cornell University.

My brother Dick married Pat, and they had four children. Dick became the top Allstate Insurance sales agent in Indiana and eventually he and Pat were the proud owners of an exotic fish and aquarium shop.

My brother Paul became a respected Deputy Sheriff.

The forever entrepreneur, my brother Jim asked me to be his best man at his wedding and went on to own an office supply business, an ice cream parlor, and various real estate investments.

My mother, after putting her children who wanted to go to college through, entered college herself at 63, earned a master's degree, and well into her late eighties was heading the child guidance counseling services for the Catholic Diocese of Fort Wayne, Indiana.

My daughter and I took her out to lunch a few months before she passed. I asked her how she was doing.

My mother graduates from college at 66.

She set her fork down and reflected. "You know, I'm finding my memory much kinder than the mirror," she said. My mother lived to 93.

What I thought was a story of *rich man, poor man* in my senior year of high school turned out to be something else. My parents were in fact well off. They just made a decision to choose a simple life so they could keep their promises back in New York State. In the course of my senior year and the year after, they paid 100 percent of the debts they owed as the result of my father's failed business venture, Distelfink. Character, to my parents, was not riding the backs of others. They moved to Fort Wayne with the prospects of my father becoming a full partner with his good friend and baker, Mr. Forks, who owned the Holsum Bakery in Fort Wayne.

My father paid cash for a modest home on Belle Avenue in Fort Wayne and sent me a bus ticket to come up from Xavier University, and instructed me to "build all the bookshelves I could fit in the place, for your mother." My father never got to be Mr. Forks's partner. During a routine doctor's visit, Mr. Forks was given a shot of penicillin. It turned out he was allergic to penicillin. He died in the ambulance on the way to the hospital.

My father managed the Holsum Bakery in Fort Wayne until he was 65—and he and my mother were at ease knowing they had managed to pay all the creditors in New York State. He made and sold frozen "Pop's Pizza" pizzas to restaurants and lived to the age of 71. More than 2,000 people came to his funeral at St. Mary's, back in Cortland, New York. He was forever Big Mike.

THE BOY AND THE BIG WHITE ROCK

When my oldest sister, Mary, was in her late eighties we had a sibling argument about our father. She was convinced he was only ever a bakery employee, and that he never respected the cars the company would let him use. "He'd pull you kids on sleds behind all around the fields and pastures with his cars. The cars were for work, not play."

I listened to my older sister, but I held my conviction that my dad was a bigger and smarter man than how my educated elder siblings painted him.

I remembered something that happened to me before I moved from Milwaukee to Cincinnati to start my basketball scholarship at Xavier University. My father drove me to the Greyhound Bus depot and told me that if I ever needed money to "Go into any big bakery anywhere and tell them you're Big Mike's son."

When I got to Cincinnati, out of curiosity, I made it a point of going into the Klostermann Bakery and then into the Rubel's Bakery and told the owners I was Big Mike's son—in just those words. Both Mr. Klostermann and Mr. Rubel shook my hand, welcomed me to Cincinnati and told me a time card would be available for me, and that anytime I needed extra money to just clock in, day or night.

Big Mike was everything I ever believed he was. He was real. But being bigger than life was one thing—worth being paid enough to pay off $100,000 in debts (one million in today's dollars) in just two years was quite another.

The numbers added up. It was possible for a bakery to pay him enough to pay off his $100,000 in debts, but was he worth that much? What was his secret to going into an established, successful bakery and making its sales jump?

As I thought back to my many road trips with him in upstate New York, I remember him telling me his secret.

"Most bakers think their job is to sell to grocers—to stop in from time to time and put loaves of bread and packages of buns on a grocers' shelves. It's a mindset, son. My customer isn't the grocery store. My customer is the homemaker who enjoys my baked goods in their kitchen and on their table. My aim is to please the customer. You can't please the homemaker with empty grocery store shelves."

I remember one time my father had me come up from Cincinnati for an entire Fourth of July weekend and stand at the bread rack in the largest grocery store in Fort Wayne, Indiana. He asked me to keep the bread racks filled, and there would always be a bakery truck outside with more. While competitors' racks were emptied by noon on Saturday—and throughout the three-day weekend—I used at least eighty cartons of bread and buns to keep our racks filled all the way through the Fourth. That alone would have tripled his baker's sales for the weekend over any of his competitors. That theory alone would have made him enough to pay his debts.

In Milwaukee he had trucks lined up at the Milwaukee Braves stadium for hot dog and hamburger buns for games starting months before the world series. Hotdog and hamburger sales would double and triple per game. Same in Fort Wayne Indiana for Holsum bakery. My father had a tractor trailer of buns waiting at the Indianapolis Speedway stadium for all the racing trial events and the Indianapolis 500 race. "I don't think of kitchens running out of hotdogs. I think about baseball or racing fans not being able to enjoy a hotdog or hamburger because of no buns—the full experience of being a fan," my father would say.

Big Mike was bigger than life ... and he thought bigger than life. I called the New York State and county clerks, and asked the officials to pull legal documents and records. Lo and behold, my father was everything I had dreamed he was. He was a full and equal founding partner in a bakery founded in 1929. The Depression started in 1930 and so did my father's bakery. From that day until the day in the 1950s when he sold his interest, that bakery baked and sold 82,000 loaves of bread a day, 365 days a year. He bought us a county park—during the Depression.

As to Delphi Falls, my mother and father had given a lawyer power of attorney to sell it to help pay debts. The attorney—after receiving a handwritten letter from my mother that *all* the Distelfink creditors had been paid in full—wrote a personal check for $6,000, paid the Delphi Falls mortgage off, took ownership of the property, and sold it for $32,000 to someone, keeping all the money. With power of attorney, he broke no law, but may he roast in hell.

Delphi Falls Park, my childhood home, is a county park again.

The White Rock, upper right on cliff.

The big white rock? To me the big white rock will always be testimony to the fundamentals my mother and father taught me. It's not a waste to think things through before acting in haste. What better place to think than the big white rock?

Just after the turn of the century (2009) the white rock fell from the cliff into the creek below. It has been moved into a permanent home in a museum. The big white rock is on display at the Pompey Museum campus, in Pompey, New York.

www.ingramcontent.com/pod-product-compliance
Lightning Source LLC
Jackson TN
JSHW010152300425
83547JS00026B/148